Homeland and
Philosophy

Popular Culture and Philosophy® Series Editor: George A. Reisch

For full details of all **Popular Culture and Philosophy**® books, visit www.opencourtbooks.com.

Popular Culture and Philosophy®

Homeland and Philosophy

For Your Minds Only

Edited by

ROBERT ARP

OPEN COURT
Chicago

Volume 85 in the series, Popular Culture and Philosophy®, edited by George A. Reisch

To order books from Open Court, call toll-free 1-800-815-2280, or visit our website at www.opencourtbooks.com.

Open Court Publishing Company is a division of Carus Publishing Company, dba Cricket Media.

Copyright © 2014 by Carus Publishing Company, dba Cricket Media

First printing 2014

Printed and bound in the United States of America.

ISBN: 978-0-8126-9857-2

Library of Congress Control Number: 2014947500

Contents

Contents

It's What Keeps Us Watching *Homeland*

ROBERT ARP

When I watched the pilot episode of *Homeland*, the al-Qaeda component reminded me of where I was when 9/11 occurred. It's crystal clear in my memory: I was in grad school at Saint Louis University, getting ready to go teach Introduction to Philosophy, standing in the kitchen of my home on Hampstead Street in St. Louis, looking out the back window at the flowers we planted in the spring, having just placed my dishes in the dishwasher, and my wife called me from her first-grade classroom, and said, "Turn on the news. A plane just flew into the World Trade Center."

I watched the second tower collapse in near-real time on TV—it was 9:28 A.M. Central Standard Time.

Like most everyone else, I was deeply depressed that day and for several days after; then angry, then sad again, then angry again. Because of these emotions (and I'm sure I'm not alone in thinking this), the Islamist jihadist extremism of al-Qaeda—complete with the terrorist activities associated with it—is what initially attracted me to *Homeland*.

There's the obvious question of the nature and ethics of terrorism in *Homeland*, but things got deep pretty quickly as I was able to pinpoint numerous philosophical themes in the show the more I watched. And I'm not alone. The authors in this book present some straightforward philosophical topics and arguments picked out from *Homeland* stories, but they also have used characters, ideas, and plot lines as a springboard into some of their own philosophizing. The goal in this book is pretty simple: we want to use *Homeland* as a way to bring some philosophy to you, the reader, as well as bring you to some philosophy.

Do We Need God to Be Moral?

The very first philosophical problem that came to mind while I was watching the pilot episode of *Homeland* has to do with whether some kind of god can act as the foundation for moral behavior or even ethics itself. I ponder this with my students in the ethics and philosophy of religion courses I teach. After all, the terrorists who flew planes into the Twin Towers of the World Trade Center, other members of al-Qaeda, the Taliban, al Shabaab, Hamas, Hezbollah, and many others—just like Nazir, Hamid, Brody, and other jihadists in the show—believed they were doing the will of Allah, their god. And, of course, there are plenty of people in this world, especially most Americans, who think that the garden-variety jihadist actually is doing the will of Satan rather than Allah!

I want to make clear here, as I will later, that I'm referring to *Islamist jihadism* and (quasi-)equating *that* with terrorist activities, which is wholly fair given the fanatical ideological activities of such groups—suicide bombings, bombings, firebombings, assassinations, wholesale murders of innocents, commonplace beheadings, torture, hijacking of planes, overtaking of facilities, unjust imprisonments—as well as tenets and statements that anyone can read (and listen to) in newspapers, blogs, on websites, and other on-line media. I am *not* equating, in any way, this jihadism with the gentle, decent, pious, self-controlled, cultured, and intelligent *typical* followers of Islam who make up the overwhelming majority of adherents of this religion.

Gremlin Gods?

However, speaking as a philosopher here, there are a few things that count against attempts to ground ethics in any god whatsoever, and there are also problems—many would argue obvious ones—with the garden-variety jihadist basing ethical decisions in their specific conception of a god.

First, if what you mean by *god* is some kind of non-physical, non-sensible, immaterial, divine entity (or entities) that is beyond scientific detection, then you're going to have a heck of a time *proving* the existence of such a being (or beings) to the rational mind in the first place. A god has to be shown to *exist*, obviously, in order to be a source or ground for morality. You wouldn't want to believe, "The Great and Powerful Gremlins who are keeping the universe in existence have commanded me to do X, and so I must do X" or "In His infinite wisdom, the Superlative Being, Proteus Maximus, has ordained that all should do Y—yeah, verily, we shall do Y." Why not? Because I just made up these beings as I type right now.

Sure, you can use religious faith and say that your faith shows that god exists, but by definition religious faith is a belief in something that defies rational provability and explanation. You might be able to convince stupid, gullible, emotionally distraught, irrational, zealous, mentally handicapped, or mentally ill people—as well as folks who already blindly believe in a god—that some god exists, but . . . You get the point.

Will the Real God Please Stand Up?

Also, there are so many different conceptions of god and gods, not only would you have to prove that god exists, but you'd also have to show that *your god* is the really, truly existing god worth worshipping and listening to, while everyone else's conception of god is wrong and false. In other words, you'd have to *prove* your god and *disprove* any other god at the same time. "The Gremlins are false gods!" claim the Proteus Maximites; "Proteus Maximus doesn't exist. He's a lie!" shout the followers of the Gremlins.

Heck, never mind all of the conceptions of god viewed through the vast multitude of the World's religions—Judaism and all of its varieties versus Islam and all of its varieties versus Hinduism and all of its varieties—just think about all of the numerous, different, often-competing conceptions of the Christian god alone! Catholic Christians, for example, think their version of god demands that folks do good works (the so-called *corporal and spiritual works of mercy* like "feed the hungry" and "instruct the ignorant") as well as have faith in Jesus Christ in order to be saved and get into Heaven, while your standard evangelical Protestant Christian thinks their version of god ultimately demands faith in Jesus Christ *only* to secure a place in Paradise. Maybe that's why your typical televangelist can be a lecherous, adulterous, greedy, egomaniacal, megalomaniacal prick, but still "be saved." Thank you, Jeeeeeeeeesus!

I Thought God's Supposed to Be Good?

Speaking of different conceptions of god, the Christian god is different from the god of Islam in at least one important way: Muslims generally think that the Christian trinity (one God in three persons—Father, Son, and Holy Spirit) is actually an abomination and insult to Allah, who is a solitary, unique being. Jesus was, at best, a prophet of Allah. (Christians usually respond by noting that they don't believe in three gods, just one, but that this one god is made manifest in three ways, but we'll put that debate aside here.) But even in Islam, just as in Christianity and other world religions, there are seemingly inconsistent ideas about Allah and especially about the will of Allah. The conception of Allah fostered by the Islamist jihadist extremist, like we find with al-Qaeda, is only one conception in Islam; in fact, most other sects of Islam don't subscribe to such extremism and have condemned jihadist terrorist activities, to include 9/11. In a public statement just a few days after the 9/11 attacks, the highest-ranking *mufti* (Sunni Islamic scholar) in Saudi Arabia noted:

> Firstly, the recent developments in the United States including hijacking planes, terrorizing innocent people, and shedding blood,

constitute a form of injustice that cannot be tolerated by Islam, which views them as gross crimes and sinful acts. Secondly, any Muslim who is aware of the teachings of his religion and who adheres to the directives of the Holy Qur'an and the sunnah (the teachings of the Prophet Muhammad) will never involve himself in such acts, because they will invoke the anger of God Almighty and lead to harm and corruption on Earth.

The last point actually counts against the garden-variety jihadist trying to ground their moral decisions in their own conception of god. All mainstream religions, as well as most sects of Islam, condemn the actions of al-Qaeda as evil and in no way, shape, or form grounded in a legitimate conception of a *good* god. Virtually any religion is going to view god as good, and this good god would never condone, endorse, or command terrorist activities like 9/11 where so many innocent folks—close to three thousand, including around sixty Muslims, by the way—were killed.

Religions from the East and West throughout human history have endorsed the killing of innocents as a by-product or unfortunate collateral damage of doing some *greater* good, as in a just war, no doubt. During World War II, when the US dropped bombs on Nazi military installations and unintentionally killed German civilians who happened to be nearby, it was of course tragic, but most think that the action wasn't sinister or immoral. (The A bombs on Hiroshima and Nagasaki in Japan are arguably something different.) And Osama Bin Laden surely thought of the 9/11 attacks as a holy war. Less than a week after the attacks, a tape featuring Bin Laden has him stating: "America has been hit by Allah at its most vulnerable point, destroying, thank God, its most prestigious buildings."

But 9/11 was different in that: 1. there was no conventional war waged, despite Bin Laden's belief in a "holy war"; 2. given that there was no conventional war, the World Trade Center couldn't be considered a military installation, and even if there was a conventional war being fought, the WTC *still* couldn't ever be considered a military installation given that it's an economic center; 3. Muslims were knowingly, willingly, deliberately killed with Bin Laden himself saying in an interview after the attacks, "Islamic law says that Muslims should not stay long in the land of infidels, and those Muslims had stayed too long."

You'd Be Wise to Choose (A)

Followers of Bin Laden and al-Qaeda see 9/11 and other terrorist activities as necessary in the holy war that is waged where the World will be divided into (A) the followers of Allah and (B) the infidels, with the followers of Allah directed by this god to "take up arms and kill those who are infidels." This command from god is worse than any homicide or even genocide—it's *humanity*-o-cide with some seven billion infidels dead in the end. Your standard Muslim wishes that all humans would "see the light" and become Muslim. Your standard Islamist jihadist extremist wishes that, too, but will make damn sure you're dead if you don't convert!

But, if "taking up arms and killing those who are infidels" is the will of Allah, commanded by him, then it makes sense to conclude either that the terrorists have the wrong conception of god, because a good god wouldn't command this, or god really is evil in commanding atrocities like 9/11 (there are other options, too, just so you know I'm not putting forward a false dilemma/dichotomy).

God Seems . . . Well . . . Pretty Goddamned Evil at Times!

When you look at any standard scripture from one of the World's religions—the Old Testament of Jews, the New Testament of Christians, the Qur'an of Muslims, the Vedas of Hindus—you will find instances of some god commanding things that seem to run counter to our moral intuitions. Let's consider one story most of us probably know.

Imagine walking down the street one day and you see an old guy lifting his knife over his head as he's about to kill some kid tied up over a rock. You run up to him in the nick of time and stop him from completing the deed. You then ask him in astonishment, "Why are you doing this?" and he says, "This is my son, and God commanded me to do this." Not only would you think he's crazy, but you'd have to think that any god who commanded this was him/her/itself evil. Most of us give god a pass here saying something like, "God was testing Abraham, and Abraham didn't kill Isaac anyway." But this misses the point: Abraham *would have killed* Isaac if God commanded it, *and let him do it*, and this seems as morally evil as any crazy Islamist jihadist extremist who claims to be doing the will of Allah.

Besides the Abraham and Isaac story from Genesis 22, consider these snippets from the Old Testament scriptures of the god of the Israelites commanding, condoning, co-ordinating, or himself creating all kinds of heinous acts:

Genesis 6:11–17 and 7:11–24. Think hard about this one, a story we kind of take for granted. God isn't pleased with how wicked humans are and decides to wipe out all living things in a massive world flood, minus Noah's family and two of every species. Not everyone could possibly be wicked, and innocent animals can't be considered wicked, so what's up with that? It seems like murder (totally unjustified and unjust killing). By the way, there are at least three science-based empirical problems to note here: 1. there's no way that it could rain for forty days and forty nights without stripping virtually all oxygen from the air, killing living things under the storm clouds, to include Noah, his family, and all the two-by-two animals; 2. for water to have covered the entire Earth, there would need to be *no* mountainous regions (which is false, given the evidence from geologists) or else the water would need to be as high as Mount Everest (which is impossible given the composition and size of the Earth); 3. finally, Noah's ark would have to have been the friggin' size of the continent of Africa (!!!) to hold two of every species—complete with its own ocean to hold the sea creatures—and even at its specified size of 300 cubits long (450 feet), 50 cubits wide

(75 feet), and 30 cubits high (45 feet) it would have fallen apart in the water, or may not have even floated at all under the weight of so many animals on board. There's more problems if you take such a story literally. Massive flooding that appears to be worldwide from the limited worldview of those folks living in that area, many can believe, and there's scientific evidence for this; however, *actual worldwide flooding*—as fervent fundamentalists would have us believe—no way.

Exodus 12:29–30. "At midnight the Lord struck down all the firstborn in Egypt, from the firstborn of Pharaoh, who sat on the throne, to the firstborn of the prisoner, who was in the dungeon, and the firstborn of all the livestock as well. Pharaoh and all his officials and all the Egyptians got up during the night, and there was loud wailing in Egypt, for there was not a house without someone dead." Really? Why did it have to be all of the innocent first-born children? Even if the first-born children were men or women, it's still murder. You could argue that the Egyptians were slaveholders of the Israelites, so they had it coming; but, again, innocent folks? And perpetrated *directly* by the Lord Himself? Wow.

Judges 21:10–11. "And the congregation sent thither twelve thousand men of the valiantest, and commanded them, saying, Go and smite the inhabitants of Jabeshgilead with the edge of the sword, with the women and the children. And this is the thing that ye shall do, Ye shall utterly destroy every male, and every woman that hath lain by man." But they kept all of the virgins, just so you know. Here, the so-called congregation is committing nearly wholesale genocide, apparently interpreting their god's will.

1 Samuel 15:3. Here, the Israelites' god commands, "Now go and smite Amalek, and utterly destroy all that they have, and spare them not; but slay both man and woman, infant and suckling, ox and sheep, camel and ass." This is wholesale genocide! What could possibly justify this? In tribal, ethnic societies that exist today—in Africa, Asia, and South Asia, for instance—this may be commonplace to wipe out, or want to wipe out, some race; but if those of us who are rational realize that this is wholly evil (and impractical, too, because it leads only to more destruction) with our limited intellects, you would think that the Almighty Himself in His Infinite Wisdom would have realized this already!

2 Samuel 5:25, 2 Kings 6:18–19, 10:17. First, God tells David to wipe out the Philistines, "And David did as the Lord commanded him, and smote the Philistines . . ." Next, Elisha prayed to God to make the Aramean army blind, "So the Lord struck them with blindness as Elisha had asked." Elisha is able to trick the poor blind bastards afterwards, leading them into Samaria. Then, when Jehu gets to Samaria, "he slew all that remained unto Ahab in Samaria, till he had destroyed him, according to the saying of the Lord, which he spake to Elijah."

Isaiah 13:15, 14:21–22. Raping and pillaging and murder of innocents, oh my! The god of the Israelites commands all of this against the enemies of the Israelites: "Every one who is captured will be thrust through; all who are caught will fall by the sword. Their infants will be dashed to pieces before their eyes; their houses will be plundered, their wives will be ravished. Prepare slaughter for his children for the iniquity of their fathers."

Jeremiah 16:4. The Lord says: "They shall die grievous deaths; they shall not be lamented; neither shall they be buried; but they shall be as dung upon the face of the earth: and they shall be consumed by the sword, and by famine; and their carcasses shall be meat for the fowls of heaven, and for the beasts of the earth."

Ezekiel 6:12–13. The Lord says: "They will fall by the sword, famine and plague. He that is far away will die of the plague, and he that is near will fall by the sword, and he that survives and is spared will die of famine. So will I spend my wrath upon them. And they will know I am the Lord, when the people lie slain among their idols around their altars, on every high hill and on all the mountaintops, under every spreading tree and every leafy oak."

Ezekiel 6:12–13. The Lord commands: "Slay old men outright, young men and maidens, little children and women."

Hosea 13:16. The Lord commands: "They shall fall by the sword: their infants shall be dashed in pieces, and their women with child shall be ripped up."

And the list goes on and on and on . . .

Ironically enough, we're told that God's "mercy endureth forever" (1 Chronicles 16:34) and that the "Lord is good to all, and his tender mercies are over all his works" (Psalms 145:9)—but wait, such mercy and love seems to be reserved only for the Israelites who are "servants continuing wholeheartedly in your way" (2 Chronicles 6:14). Aw shucks!

Atrocity with God's Backing

The crazy and immoral things that gods seem to be commanding folks in this world to do—right now and throughout history—gets me to think that these folks are just making up a god to justify their evil actions. Hitler, Stalin, Mao Zedong, and virtually every major world religion—Crazy Christians at times, too, "The Inquisition, let's begin / The Inquisition, look out sin . . ."—have used a god to justify horrible, unmentionable deeds (for a start, check out "When God Sanctions Killing: Effect of Scriptural Violence on Aggression" in the Volume 18, Number 3, 2007, issue of *Psychological Science*). Think again about the Abraham and Isaac story: we all know that what god commanded Abraham to do was downright evil. Think also about the other examples from the Old Testament I gave where god is smiting and commanding other to smite, as well as rape and pillage. Why even think that a god that wills us to do evil things even exists in the first place?

Or, could it be that I really don't need some god or gods to ground my moral decisions because I can use reason, scientific investigation, historical precedent, and other human capacities to ground morality? After all, it was reason that led me to see the moral inconsistencies in a supposed law or command of god in the first place. Why should I have a god in my belief system when I can see *on my own* that morality requires rational consistency, fairness, respect for persons, and other moral principles? And did you notice that there was no mention whatsoever of a god in the previous question?

What I've tried to do in this introduction is give you a little taste of the kind of philosophizing you'll find in this book. I mentioned a hot-button topic in ethics and philosophy of religion, but you'll also see some metaphysics, epistemology, political philosophy, and logic as you read these pages. I invite you to start reading. In the words of Saul from Season Three's "Big Man in Tehran," "Let's get it done. Do it now . . ."

I

Who *Are* You?

1
You're Responsible Today for the You of Yesterday

JASON IULIANO

When you wake up in the morning, how do you know that you're not someone else? Do you stand in front of the mirror and loudly affirm, "I am ME"? Do you think hard about the night to see if an imposter tried to take over your body while you were sleeping? Or perhaps you check your mental catalog to see if Pop Tarts are still your favorite breakfast food. Imagine waking up one morning to find that you can't wait to down a jar of pickled herrings. (Germans love having this for breakfast. Disgusting, right?) Surely any person who wanted that for breakfast couldn't be you anymore!

In the pilot episode of *Homeland*, Helen Walker asks Sergeant Brody if he was present when her husband died. Brody pauses and pictures himself beating Tom Walker to death. Only then does he reply, "No."

"Brody, you lying son of a bitch!" you likely screamed at the TV. But were you right to do so? Is the Sergeant Brody who answered Helen Walker's question *the same person* who savagely beat Tom Walker and remembers (albeit incorrectly) killing him? Is it possible that the Brody who left for war is a distinct person from the Brody who returned home? In other words, did you falsely accuse Brody of murdering his wartime pal?

As you can see, we need to get into some pretty fascinating philosophical puzzles. We have to dig to the core of what makes you, *you*, and why the *you* of today is morally responsible for the actions of the you of yesterday.

Resolving these questions will help us figure out whether 2011 Brody is morally responsible for the actions of 2003 Brody, and likewise whether it makes sense to praise 2011 Brody for the heroic military service of 2003 Brody. We'll also get to the bottom of whether Brody lied to Helen Walker. But first . . .

What if I Told You You're Gonna Be Tortured?

Whoosh. A brutish hand wrenches the captors' hood off your head. Bright white light blinds you. You blink rapidly, attempting to acclimatize yourself to the surroundings. "Where am I?" you think to yourself. "Who are these people? What do they want with me?" As these questions race through your mind, a black silhouette steps in front of you. A few moments pass and your eyes begin to find purchase. The silhouette is slowly transformed into an Arab man with glasses and a greying beard. There's a look of pity on his face. "Hello, I am Abu Nazir. It is time we finally met. You have information that I want, and I will get it from you one way or another." You see an assortment of torture devices (an electric drill, pliers, a screwdriver, and even a blowtorch) on the table next to Nazir and tremble noticeably. Before you can protest or dwell too long on the torture that awaits, someone else approaches from behind and knocks you unconscious with a blow to the head.

First, the good news (there's bad news later, so don't get too excited): This scene wasn't happening just now. Rather, you were watching it unfold on a video monitor. The CIA agent sitting next to you explains that this is one possible path your life will take. She reiterates that the top-secret future-predicting machine used to generate this video is just that, a *prediction* machine. "It can't tell the future with absolute certainty. There are always alternatives. This is just a likely outcome." She looks down at her clipboard and asks, "With that in mind, how does your future make you feel?"

"Terrified!" you shout back. "I don't want to be tortured. I don't even know who Abu Nazir is. What could he possibly want with me?"

The CIA agent declines to answer your question, instead queuing up another video on the future predicting machine.

Are You Really You?

In this video, everything seems the same. The same brutish hand tearing off your hood. The same blinding light. The same Arab gentleman fading into view. The only difference comes at the end. The pitying look is gone, replaced by one of joy and gratitude. "Hello, I am Abu Nazir," the man begins. "It is time we finally met. I want to thank you for your service. By detonating the bomb at the State of the Union address, you have done so much to advance our cause." You respond, "I am only too happy to serve you in destroying the American infidels."

Now, the bad news (I told you it was coming): this is the other path your life could take. Reading from her clipboard, the CIA agent again asks, "How does your future make you feel?"

"That's not *my* future!" you insist. "I am not that kind of person. I would *never* do something like that. I love my country."

"But that person in the video is you, isn't it?"

"Yes, I mean NO. The person looks like me—albeit a few years older and a bit more weathered, but that's not me. I don't know who that person is, but it certainly isn't me."

The CIA agent presses you harder on this point. "If that future comes to be, that person in the video will have all of the memories that you currently hold. That individual will remember kissing your first crush, driving your first car, eating your favorite food . . . Everything you've done in your life, that person will remember doing, too. You both have the same body. You both have the same memories. How can you deny that the person in the video is you?"

You think for a while and try to put your finger on the reason. Eventually, you come to the conclusion that there is something about the second person's essential character that is incompatible with your own. It is something so fundamental that it cuts to the very core of your personhood.

After viewing the first clip, you felt concern not only for the individual in the video but also for yourself. You believed the two persons to be one and the same and feared that that person's torture would be your torture. You likely felt self-concern for the individual because your essential characters were similar. The second video elicited a very different response. Instead of identifying the individual as yourself, you immediately disclaimed any sort of connection. You doggedly insisted that the person in the video must be someone else. You would not murder hundreds of innocent Americans. Only a person with an entirely different fundamental nature could commit such a terrible act. The only fear you felt might have been fear of the loss of your own personal identity and the subsequent transformation into the monster in the video. Instead of identifying the individual as yourself, you likely lamented the loss of your current personal identity.

Multiple Brody Disorder

What would Brody have said if the CIA had sat him down in 2003 and showed him these videos? Surely, he, too, would have denied being the same person as the one who colluded with Abu Nazir to kill hundreds of Americans. Nonetheless, in 2011, Brody did just that.

In fact, Brody lived through events very similar to those that occurred in both of these videos. On May 19th 2003, he was captured along the Syrian border by Saddam Hussein's forces. After being sold to al-Qaeda commander Abu Nazir, he was systematically tortured for five years and held captive for eight. By the time of his release in 2011, Brody had been transformed from a proud American soldier into a terrorist operative determined to destroy the nation that he once dedicated his life to protecting.

The extent of Brody's change is fully revealed in the Season One finale ("Marine One"). In that episode, Brody straps a bomb to his chest, infiltrates the panic room where numerous important politicians are hiding, and goes so far as to press the button to detonate the bomb. Only by happenstance, the trigger fails. The man who had pledged his life to defending America had just tried to assassinate many of its top government officials.

While interrogating the sergeant, Carrie Mathison hypothesizes how this dramatic change might have come about. "[Abu Nazir] systematically pulled you apart, Brody. Piece by piece until there was nothing left but pain. And then he relieved the pain. And he put you back together again as someone else" ("Q&A"). It's perhaps not surprising that Carrie would draw this distinction between pre- and post-brainwashed Brody. After all, she has personal identity issues of her own (But more on that later). For now, what's interesting is her identification of Brody as two separate persons. These "Brodys" are linked by body and psychological continuity, but nonetheless, Carrie believes there are two of them: the American soldier who went off to war and the terrorist operative who returned home. In making this observation, Carrie has employed the narrative theory of personal identity.

So, what exactly is narrative identity? Well, that's hard to say, so first let me start by saying what it isn't. The theory is not concerned with physical sameness. There are a variety of philosophical accounts that use physical sameness as a launching point, but the most popular of these conceptions is known as the biological criterion. So, you're the same person if you have the same body. Proponents of this view argue that we are essentially human animals. Although the biological account does an excellent job of identifying the same physical thing, it does a less than stellar job of identifying the correct object of our moral ascriptions. To see why, we must return to Abu Nazir's hideout.

Nazir the Mad Scientist

Let's suppose that, after Brody and Walker arrive at his compound, Nazir straps them into two chairs and places a series of electrodes on their heads. He tells them that he's going to download their psychologies—all their memories, beliefs, desires, fears, and other mental states—into a computer. He will then upload Brody's psychology into Walker's body and Walker's psychology into Brody's body. (Hey, it's possible; Nazir is an evil terrorist mastermind, after all.)

Nazir undertakes the experiment, and when Brody's body awakens, it thinks he is Tom Walker. The reverse goes for Walker's body. Nazir returns the two soldiers to their families. Which body goes where? My intuition (and likely yours) says that Brody's body should go to Walker's family and vice versa. There seems to be something essential that is contained in our psychological states. The biological criterion misses the mark here. It holds that Brody's body should go back to Brody's family and Walker's body should go back to Walker's family. Brody and Walker are essentially biological (not psychological) organisms, so who they are can be determined wholly by reference to biological continuity. According to the biological theory, their bodies have not changed, so neither have their essential beings. Brody and Walker are the same individuals they've always been. I don't know about you, but to me this analysis seems deeply mistaken.

Narrative identity theorists reject the idea that our biological properties define us. Instead, they argue that there is something essential to our psychology. We are essentially persons, not human animals, and our personhood is determined by our psychological states. Narrative identity theorists, however, are not alone in maintaining this position. Supporters of what is known as the psychological criterion have also staked out this camp. However, the precise psychological features that they emphasize are quite different than those that the narrative identity theorist accepts as critical. In the next case, Carrie's personal identity crisis will help us sort out the difference between these two theories.

Carries as Far as the Eye Can See

At the age of twenty-two, Carrie was diagnosed with bipolar disorder. To keep her illness in check, she takes the antipsychotic medication Clozapine. To hold onto her security clearance and job, Carrie has kept the condition a secret from nearly everyone around her. She even gets her sister to write prescriptions, so the CIA won't find out. Unfortunately, this causes a bit of a problem when Carrie is knocked unconscious by a briefcase bomb ("Representative Brody"). In the following episode ("The Vest"), we find her awake several days later in a hospital room. She is babbling to the nurses about how important it is for her to have a green pen. Before long, it's clear that the absence of her antipsychotic medication and the traumatic injury have caused Carrie to spiral into a manic state.

When Saul visits her in the hospital, he immediately senses that something is wrong and bluntly tells her, "You're not yourself." At that time, Carrie rejects the notion. However, in the following season ("Beirut Is Back"), while reflecting upon her mental changes, Carrie admits that she's a different person, stating, "Look, the way I am now, I wouldn't trust me either. But the Carrie who recruited [Fatima]. That one I believe."

This example helps us get at the core difference between the psychological criterion and the narrative identity theory. Proponents of the first theory would say that Saul and Carrie are clearly mistaken. Carrie is the same person before the briefcase bomb, after she enters her manic state, and even after she undergoes electroshock therapy ("Marine One"). They base this reasoning on the fact that all of these iterations of Carrie have high degrees of psychological connectedness with each other. By this, they mean that there are a significant number of overlapping memories, intentions, beliefs, and other mental states. Indeed, by and large, this is true of Carrie at each of the points in time. They all have very similar beliefs, similar intentions, and similar memories of Carrie's life—the electroshock therapy eliminated some short-term memories, but most remained intact. Despite this, there seems to be something different about Carrie at each of these three stages. Saul and even Carrie, herself, acknowledge this.

The narrative theory of identity gets at this difference by focusing on how actions are incorporated into the self-told story of your life. The theory maintains that you can only claim ownership of actions that fit together into the coherent narrative that is your life. Experiences are not a person's unless and until they have been incorporated into that person's evolving life story. Under the narrative account, our lives are akin to novels. If a past person performs an action that is antithetical to his current fundamental nature or cannot be incorporated into the story of his life, we must question whether that action can be properly attributable to the present person.

A Bit Touchy-Feely

If you're thinking, "That sounds a damn bit touchy-feely," you're right. It is. But the interesting thing is that this theory resolves many of the problems that plague competing theories. Indeed, narrative identity seems to be the theory that best captures our practical concerns, such as when we should anticipate our survival, when we should have self-concern for a future individual, and when we should bear moral responsibility.

Suppose that Carrie has to decide whether to undergo a new experimental procedure to eliminate her bipolar disorder. The doctors tell Carrie that there are three likely outcomes: 1. the procedure leaves her in a permanent vegetative state; 2. the procedure cures her of bipolar disorder but changes her character to such a degree that she will be unrecognizable to anyone who currently knows her; and 3. the procedure is a resounding success, and she both is cured of her bipolar disorder and retains her present personality.

In which of these three scenarios can Carrie reasonably anticipate surviving? Of course, her body will survive all three, but does that necessarily mean Carrie the person will survive all three? The biological criterion says *yes*. Her body is still ticking, so Carrie has survived. The psychological criterion says *no* to scenario one (her psychological states have been eliminated) but *yes* to two and three (her psychological states are connected and continuous). Finally, the narrative identity theorist would argue that Carrie the person only survives in the third case.

Because her fundamental personality and character is only preserved in the third situation, that is the only one in which Carrie survives. If you were Carrie, would you go through with the procedure?

Debriefing

Now back to the original questions that led us on this exploration of personal identity. Did Brody lie to Helen Walker? If you answered "Yes," you're hopeless. I give up. Just kidding. No matter which way you go, you're in good philosophical company.

Proponents of the biological criterion and psychological criterion maintain that he did lie. Because his physical body survived the torture, 2011 Brody is the same person as 2003 Brody under the biological criterion. Likewise, because a sufficient number of mental states have been passed along from 2003 Brody to 2011 Brody, the psychological criterion of personal identity is also satisfied. However, because Brody's fundamental nature has changed and the tenets and beliefs he holds in 2011 are completely at odds with those he held in 2003, the narrative identity theory argues that we should treat Brody as two separate persons. We shouldn't praise or blame 2011 Brody for the actions of 2003 Brody. They are separate persons with separate identities.

Don't you wish you could play that card? "Honey, *I* didn't leave the toilet seat up. That was a different person." However, I guess the whole torture thing and becoming a terrorist operative might not be worth the tradeoff.

2
Double Agents and Multiple Identities

TALIA MORAG

Brody is a Marine, a congressman, a husband, a father, a friend, a Muslim, a follower of Abu Nazir, a CIA double agent, Carrie's lover. But who is Brody? Where do his loyalties lie?

He spends the first season of *Homeland* constructing and nurturing all these roles and by the end of the second season he is left with very few. Carrie is a CIA agent, a bipolar patient, Saul's protégé, and Brody's lover. But can she manage to sustain this situation with all its conflicts?

We all describe ourselves through such labels. You are a friend, a lover, a child, a parent, married or de-facto, single or divorced, you are a teacher, a liberal, a volunteer in the neighborhood watch, a bridge player. These are the labels we put on our résumé or on a dating website. This is how we introduce ourselves to someone at a party. When people hear these descriptions of you they get the feeling (which is often misleading) that they know something about you, about the kinds of situations you face in your daily routine, about your place in the world.

Philosophers call these labels *practical identities*. They are the roles we play in relationships and in social groups. They are practical because our actions are often determined by them. Having roles at home and in the workplace comes with stuff we have to do, with duties and obligations. We

13

identify ourselves with these labels because they represent what and who matters to us. They say something about where we stand in life, about our general situation.

TV series often present people more or less stuck in such situations, much like in real life. The characters of a TV show may go through adventures every episode, but at the end of each episode, they are more or less the same as they were at the beginning. Their labels or practical identities, their basic situation in society, won't go through revolutions within one episode. Even one season usually won't revolutionize a character's labels. Carrie ends Season One as a mental patient, fired from the CIA. Her identity as a CIA agent has been taken away from her. But if that meant that from now on Carrie couldn't have anything to do with spying, then either *Homeland* would end or Carrie would leave the series. Carrie as an English teacher for newcomers who cooks lasagna on Thursdays (as she is presented in the beginning of Season Two) does not belong in *Homeland*. *Homeland* is a show about spies.

The Fragmented Brody

Brody's social roles and relationships don't sit together so well. In the beginning of Season Two, in "The Smile," Brody's wife is shocked to discover Brody is a Muslim. She says angrily: "I married a US Marine. This, this can't happen. You have a wife, two kids, you're a congressman in the running to be Vice President. It cannot happen! You get that, right?"

As the show demonstrates a number of times, being an American Muslim isn't a contradiction in terms. To take just one example, some of the CIA agents are Muslim and they are loyal Americans who love and sacrifice for their country. And yet Brody isn't annoyed by his wife's emotional prejudices and replies: "Yeah, Jess, I do."

Brody knows that the real issue isn't his conversion to Islam, but the fact that he is loyal to Abu Nazir, the infamous terrorist who is planning an attack on US soil. *As a follower of Abu Nazir*, he will have to kill innocent people to avenge the death of Issa, Abu Nazir's son. But *as a Marine, as a congressman*, he has duties and obligations to protect American lives. Those obligations are contradictory. Those practical identities don't cohere.

As philosopher Christine Korsgaard explains, we all feel the pressure to steer away from contradictory obligations. If who we are gives us reasons to do and not do the same thing, we feel that we have lost our moral compass. Something has gone wrong with our values if we feel under strong obligation to both kill and not kill. Those of us who want to see ourselves as doing the right thing have to find good reasons to choose one course of action over the other. We need to find a way to reconcile our obligations, to free ourselves from contradiction.

One obvious way is just to get rid of one label and the obligations that come with it. But can Brody solve his conflicts that easily? Can he just forget about Abu Nazir and Issa? Changing the labels on our "Identification Card" isn't so easy. At the heart of each practical identity is an emotional relationship with people and things we care about. It's not so easy just to decide not to care about someone or something anymore.

Gay Christians

Another strategy we can take to reconcile such dilemmas is to re-think what these roles actually mean. For example, what if I'm a Christian and also gay? Many would claim that these identities can't belong to one and the same person. But must they contradict one another? Can't we find a way to be gay Christians?

The Danish philosopher Søren Kierkegaard (1813–1855) demanded that we rethink labels used too easily to describe ourselves, labels like "Christian." Kierkegaard warned against misusing such labels to justify our actions. He insisted that we ask ourselves: What does it mean to be a Christian?

Kierkegaard didn't ask this question thinking about gay rights. But if we take his general advice, maybe we can think it through and find that being a gay Christian is a coherent possibility. We can step back from our practical identities, examine what they mean to us, and give them new or revised meaning. We can redefine ourselves without having to give up on our labels.

Such reflections can help us find peace and decide what's the right thing to do. But sometimes, we can abuse this strategy to rationalize and justify an action that we would probably go through with anyway. This is what Brody does when he records his suicide tape in Season One's "Marine 1, Part 1." He gives reasons for his actions before actually going through with them. He re-interprets what it means to be a Marine, and says that it is *as a Marine* that he is going to blow himself up in a room full of people. He isn't a "terrorist." He has not been "broken" or "brainwashed." It's his duty *as a Marine* to protect the US against enemies from within, such as the Vice President, and suicide-bomb him and his team.

He Flicked the Switch

Really? Are Marines supposed to execute people whom they judge to be war criminals and kill as many others as possible in the process? Is Brody just making himself feel better? Is he convincing himself this is the right thing to do? Brody tapes his declaration of intentions to help him go through with Abu Nazir's plan. Once the tape exists, his commitment to blow up exists. It's almost like he'd already done it.

Brody turned on the switch of the suicide vest at the end of that episode. He actually did it—and yet it didn't happen. Something went wrong with the vest. "Marine 1, Part 2" begins with Brody determined to fix the vest in the toilets. But just before he almost turns the switch on again, he's told his daughter is on the phone: "She says it's an emergency." Brody could have turned on the switch right there and then—but *as a father* he cannot refuse an urgent call from his daughter.

Brody begins the conversation still as an Abu Nazir follower, about to switch on a suicide bomb, and ends the conversation as Dana's dad, promising her to come back home. Dana cries and reminds Brody she needs him. Brody is attached to and loves his daughter, and he cares about how she sees him. He reasserts himself as a father who is there for his daughter. And he doesn't turn on the switch again. He didn't do it. Brody, the father and husband, returns home in Marine uniform.

On the tape Brody tried to show how his social roles could look like they belong together. But in reality, the Abu Nazir follower has to turn the switch on and Dana's father must not turn that switch on. These roles just don't cohere. The failing vest gave Brody the chance to be both. He both did it and didn't do it. Brody can go on living his double life juggling his divided loyalties.

Carrie and Brody in Her Eyes

Carrie may seem at first even more fragmented than Brody. She goes in and out of the CIA, in and out of mental hospitals and in and out of her love story with Brody. Carrie does not have stable labels to hang on to. Everyone can see that these practical identities don't sit together well. How can a manic-depressive be a CIA agent? How can a CIA agent have a "terrorist in her bed?" as Saul so bluntly puts it in the last episode of Season Two, "The Choice."

Society may not allow Carrie to pursue all her social roles at once, but Carrie is emotionally invested in all of them. She loves her country and is committed to defending it. She's attached to Saul. She appears to trust her manic attacks and keeps finding reasons to stop taking her meds. And she's always attracted to Brody, even when she hates him.

Weirdly enough, although society clearly disapproves, Carrie's emotional activities complement one another. As she watches Brody's life through the surveillance video, she is defending her country from an attack, indulging in a manic theory that only she understands, and she's falling in love with Brody—all at the same time.

Carrie gives up momentarily on her love to Brody when she confronts him in Season Two in the episode "New Car Smell": "You are a disgrace to your nation. You are a traitor and a terrorist." Brody really hates being called a terrorist. He is just a revisionary Marine. But who we are and how we're labeled isn't only up to us. Whether we are indeed "Marines" depends on the US Army, whether we are actually "friends" depends on other people seeing us as friends, and whether we are actually "employees" depends on having someone employing us.

From the moment Carrie confronts Brody to the very end of Season Two, Brody's practical identities, his place in the world, become increasingly fragile. Brody has been basing his social roles and relations on lies, and those lies get more and more complicated to maintain. Carrie gradually becomes Brody's only hope of a relationship without lies that can give Brody some self-respect. Carrie is always there to provide Brody with new descriptions of himself. And the very fact that she is the one coming up with those labels makes them more objective, genuine possibilities for Brody to re-describe himself.

Q&A

The first step in this dynamic occurs in the following episode, "Q&A." Carrie gives Brody a way to re-describe himself as a "good man," a man who affirms life, who loves his daughter, who "knows the difference between warfare and terrorism." She gets Brody to re-live the moment he spoke to his daughter on the phone, wearing a suicide vest, and decided to come home. As a CIA agent, Carrie gets Brody to turn from being a follower of Abu Nazir to a CIA recruit. As Brody's lover, she is turning Brody into the man she loves.

The mission to get Abu Nazir promises to salvage some of Brody's present, his life as an American, as a husband, and as a father. But when Brody's role with the CIA compromises his family life, he has no practical identity worth fighting for. This is the Brody Carrie has to face in the episode "I'll Fly Away." Without a present life to salvage, Carrie gives him a future vision of himself. She presents the mission as the grand gesture that Brody can still do and that will give him a chance to recover a place in the world.

Carrie imagines a future for Brody, where he becomes "the hero that got Abu Nazir." Brody cannot change what he did, but he could still change who he is. If he becomes that hero, Carrie reassures him, what he did, including wearing the vest or getting Carrie to hospitalize herself, will not matter so much any more. "Hero" promises to be an identity that would put all past screw-ups in a new perspective. They will just be the necessary evils on the way to heroism. Carrie imagines a new identity for Brody, "hero," that could enable her to accept him and all that he's done, that could enable her to love and have a future with him. Carrie always finds a way to continue loving Brody and protecting her country without conflict.

A Normal Future?

This is all very romantic, as long as we conveniently forget the detail that Carrie doesn't know and doesn't include in her vision of Brody. Carrie doesn't know that Brody, as the man on the tape, turned on the switch of the suicide vest. Could Carrie accept *that*? It's hard to tell. It's easier to delete some detail from your life-story if nobody knows about it. Those of us who like the idea of Carrie and Brody together prefer to turn a blind eye to that moment and are hoping that Brody can do the same. We want to see Brody become a hero—for Carrie.

That's why it's tragic to see the tape broadcasted on TV and Brody turning into the "Langley bomber" at the finale of Season Two. Brody and Carrie's fantasy of a normal future together depended on them keeping some secrets and lies about Brody's life. But the tape was always there, with the testimony of Brody's intentions to kill and attack Americans. Now, with the tape exposed, it's no longer enough that Carrie doesn't see him as a terrorist—everybody else does.

Being labeled a "terrorist" trumps all the other social roles Brody had. He is no longer a Marine or a congressman; he has no chance to have a normal life as an American or to maintain his relations with his family. He is left with no practical identity that would give him a place in the world. And Carrie? She would have to renounce her family and the CIA if she ran off with him, as a fugitive with a fake passport.

Who Is It?

Who is Brody now? Can he ever rise above the man on tape and have a role that would make his life worth living? Could Brody ever become the man that Carrie can be with? Can Season Three recover Brody as a Marine, as a father, or as Carrie's lover? The question "Who is Brody?" is open-ended. The "who is it?" of *Homeland* isn't a "whodunnit?" story that ends with the revelation of facts about Brody. Brody's identity isn't a fixed thing the show is set to expose. Brody keeps revealing as well as constructing who he is by the choices he makes and the actions he takes. This is true of Carrie too and of all the *Homeland* characters. That is what makes *Homeland*'s real-time operations so exciting to watch. *Homeland* keeps us in suspense about the motivations and the decisions of the characters involved.

The question "Who is it?" is a source of drama and suspense in our own lives as well. Most of us have much more stable practical identities than Brody or Carrie. But, as Sartre emphasized, we are not just playing the roles society gives us and we are not summaries of our past. We also have our everyday dramas, moments of choice and action, that give content to our labels. Our everyday lives, as teachers or lawyers, as family members or friends, frequently present us with new challenges. It is how each of us deals with our particular challenges that decides who we are as individuals and how our particular life-story could be told. Like Brody and Carrie, we are all "work in progress."

Homeland, as a show about spies with otherwise unstable practical identities, explores a source of drama and suspense of many TV Series. In a sense, the question "Who is it?" drives many of our favorite TV Series. When we watch shows on cops or lawyers, housewives or prison inmates, we're watching the everyday lives of others. We watch how others deal with the challenges and dilemmas of their life situations. We keep watching more episodes, not so much to see what *happens* next, but to see what our favorite characters will *do* next. We get attached to these characters as we learn what they are capable of, what kind of cops or lawyers or prison inmates they are. We keep watching with care and interest how these characters handle their social roles, how they shape who they are in their relationships.

3
My Dad the Jihadist Murderer

László Kajtár

If I had to make a list of the most awkward sex scenes that I've seen, the one in "Pilot" would take a prominent position. Jessica puts on nice lingerie for Brody's sort of homecoming-celebration sex. Yeah, the man was a prisoner of war for eight years, he must be pretty horny by now. But instead of an ideal, passionate night of re-uniting lovemaking, the "re-united" husband and wife are taken more apart by a violent act that lasts for a minute or so.

The scene is awkward in its expressiveness: it illustrates the mental damage Brody has suffered and Jessica's mistaken expectations about his homecoming. As she puts it later: "If someone had warned me how he'd look at me as if he didn't know me anymore. How violent his nightmares would be that he would attack me in his sleep, um, how he didn't know what to say to the kids those first few weeks. How hard intimacy of any kind would be for him" ("State of Independence").

Take a look at the two main characters of *Homeland*: Carrie and Brody. It's definitely not an everyday experience to see so much damage coupled up (pun intended). In Carrie's words, "no one survives intact" ("Q&A"). Carrie suffers from bipolar disorder, a mood disorder that has alternating phases: a manic and a depression phase. The manic phase is anxious, nervous, full of energy, while depression is, well, if

23

you haven't seen it around you, consider yourself lucky, and just try to recall Carrie on a bad day.

Brody suffers from a widely known mental illness: post-traumatic stress disorder (PTSD). With its main characters, not to mention Dana's suicide attempt among other things, *Homeland* paints a pretty bleak picture of people's mental health.

Let's say there is a Brody who had gone to war and there is a Brody who came back. Are the two Brodys the same person? Some would say there's a simple answer. Sure, he's the same guy, he just got some problems in his head! But maybe there's more to it.

Not a Monster?

Brody's mental disorder, PTSD, is widely known precisely because of cases of traumatized soldiers. It was called 'battle fatigue' before the time of the First World War, 'shell shock' after, and 'combat stress reaction' at the time of the Second. Brody is supposed to be thirty-eight years old in 2013, so he had spent more than one fifth of his life as a prisoner of Abu Nazir. War and captivity are traumatic enough, but Brody was forced to kill—or so he believed—his fellow soldier, Tom Walker. Brody was also subjected to continuous torture for five years and to mental manipulation for three, something we could call 'brainwashing'. It turned him into a terrorist in the hands of Abu Nazir. If you think that asking about the two Brodys is mere philosophical theorizing, then consider this: many people suffering from PTSD report that they do not feel to be the same person as before their trauma.

So what is PTSD? We seem to be acquainted with trauma-related disorders through our own experiences and through depictions in books, movies and other media. Trauma comes from the Greek word for "wound", and the default resource, the new fifth edition of the *Diagnostic and Statistical Manual of Mental Disorders* defines it as experiencing a threat of death, injury or violence or actually suffering injury or violence. However, people react differently to trauma, and only some develop a disordered reaction.

Remember what Jessica said: "How violent his nightmares would be that he would attack me in his sleep" ("State of Independence"). PTSD researchers call such nightmares and waking involuntary recollections "intrusive" since they intrude into normal sleep or awareness. If you want to see examples go back to "Grace" and you can watch Brody re-living several traumatic experiences. Brody also tries to avoid anything that would remind him of what he had to go through, like talking about it truthfully because reminders and remembering can trigger reliving the experiences. Plus Brody is always on edge. As PTSD researchers would say, he is in a hyperaroused state. Understandably, this all can lead to "impaired functioning" in different areas of one's life, and the family life of Brody suffers from it greatly. The result leaves no doubt that Brody is severely traumatized: his psyche is scarred as much as his body.

Some researchers differentiate between Type I and Type II trauma. Type I is when the trauma is single incident, while Type II is repeated or prolonged exposure. Surviving a brutal assault constitutes Type I trauma, while Brody's torture in captivity a Type II. Sometimes Type II is also called Complex PTSD, Complex because there are significant differences about the disorder in these cases. For instance, someone who suffers from Complex PTSD is more likely to go through deep personality changes than PTSD sufferers in general. As you can notice, I haven't asked whether Carrie is the same person as before. Besides being bipolar, it's clear that she's traumatized, especially by the death of her translator. But her trauma is different from Brody's, Carrie's trauma is Type I.

Brody says the following as if he was talking about himself: "Walker is not the person you think he is. He stopped being a marine the day he turned a traitor" ("Beirut Is Back"). Seeing what Brody's gone through, I'm inclined to think that, in an important sense, he is not the same person as he was before his deployment. There's also no guarantee that he can ever be the same again. Even after the CIA captures and recruits him, he still assists in killing the Vice

President. You could say that he only did it to save Carrie, but this isn't strictly true. His last words to the Vice President are: "I'm killing you" ("Broken Hearts").

Brody Pulled Apart and Put Back Together Again

So how do philosophers generally approach the issue of personal identity? Well, as you might expect, there is no consensus, and there are many questions. How can philosophy help us to understand what Brody's going through? The situation is the following: Nick Brody was deployed as a solider. Before, he had a family life and was probably a normal or average husband, if one can guess. He had been captured and he was "rescued" after eight years. Is he the same Nick Brody as before? He is now a Muslim. In the first season, and in the first episodes of the second, he was a terrorist, doing the bidding of Abu Nazir.

Even though he was probably genuinely happy to be reunited with his family, his family took a secondary role next to his secret life. He was ready to sacrifice himself in order to kill the Vice President, and later he did help killing him. He mistakenly believed himself to have killed Tom Walker, and then, at the end of Season One, he actually did. When you imagine a Nick Brody who wasn't deployed as a solider and who wasn't captured by Abu Nazir, could you also imagine him ending up like this naturally, on his own? If not, then it makes sense to ask whether the Brody before and the Brody after are the same. Right, we all go through changes in personality, people can convert to different religions or change lifestyles, and so on. However, the issue is whether these changes preserve who we are or whether we get lost along the way.

Some philosophers believe that we are first and foremost animals, and this approach is labeled "animalism." It is one of the "somatic" or body-based views. Animalists would say that Brody is an animal organism, and he has the "persistence conditions" of one. What this means is that as long as Brody's body carries out its biological functions, Brody is the same. Brody is the same organism as he was when he was a fetus, he is the same organism before the war, and he is the same when he was rescued. He would even be the same if he slipped into a coma following the Ibogaine treatment of his heroin addiction in "One Last Time." Brody lives the same biological life as long as he's alive. There is something straightforwardly true about this, and it gets even more convincing because we all know that we are animals. The issue seems to be that there is something missing. Is this all there is?

The Psychological Approach

Other philosophers are advocates of what has become known as the psychological approach, and as the label indicates, it seems to have more to do with PTSD and personality changes than animalism. A sort of default psychological approach could be based on memory, which has its source in the influential writings of the seventeenth-century empiricist, John Locke. Taking this approach, we might think that memory makes Brody the same as he was before his deployment. Brody definitely remembers his family, and so he must be the same person as he was before. If Brody, for instance, has suffered an amnesia-inducing brain injury when he was captured, he would not be the same person as before.

Others propose more nuanced versions of the psychological approach. This type of view takes psychological or mental states seriously. Beliefs, memories, intentions, desires, these are all possible psychological or mental states, and it seems that they are quite important for us as persons. Just ask yourself the question: if you lost all these, would you be the same person? The answer is not straightforward. If Brody had a vision of the future in which he as a brainwashed terrorist "takes care" of his family after his return, would he have been content with it? Would he have said "sure, that's me, he can take care of my family"? You might say that it doesn't matter, and some philosopher would agree with you, saying that the metaphysical state-of-affairs does not depend on Brody's opinion about himself.

The advocates of the psychological approach would say that in order for Brody to be the same before and after, he has to have a certain psychological relation that obtains throughout the time period. This doesn't mean that he needs to have one particular belief that carries him through the eight years of captivity. Instead, you need to look at the psychological makeup of Brody before and trace the way his beliefs, desires, intentions, and so on changed or stayed the same. Many of your beliefs, desires, and so on change during your lifetime. However, if the changes are gradual, and if there is a coherency to your psychological continuity and connectedness, then the proponent of the psychological approach would say that you are the same person. In contrast to animalism, however, Brody cannot fall into a coma, strictly speaking. If we suppose that comatose patients do not have beliefs, intentions and desires, then they cannot be identical to the persons before the coma.

The Mind-Fuck World of Abu Nazir

Philosophers generally like well-ordered and, we could say, 'normal' things. There's probably nothing a philosopher of mind likes more than a 'normal' mind. Unfortunately, as *Homeland* demonstrates forcefully, minds are often 'abnormal'. Mental disorder is most likely more pervasive on the average than we believe. Of course, Carrie's bipolar disorder and Brody's severe PTSD are not common, but they do illustrate that things can go wrong with a normal mind quite easily. These severe cases tell us something about our normal and mentally healthy minds.

If we take the psychological perspective seriously, we can't just say that Brody is the same human animal, continuing the same human life as he lived before his deployment. On the biological level, this makes sense. The Brody, kissing his wife Jessica and saying goodbye to his kids is not straightforwardly the same as the Brody, suffering and sitting in a corner of the bedroom all day after being rescued ("Grace"). As Dana says, the last true thing her dad said to her was "Good Bye" ("Game On").

Brody was captured and tortured. Abu Nazir's intention was to turn and 'brainwash' him from the beginning. After years of torture, "a man walked in and he was kind to me, and I loved him," as Brody says ("The Weekend"). It was not the kindness of the heart, but the kind of kindness that is part of a plan. In "Clean Skin," Brody's asked "to what end" he was tortured. He remembers Abu Nazir and being able to devour some fruit. "They want you to lose faith," he explains. Trauma weakens your psychic defenses. A traumatic experience creates a disruption in the normal ways of your mind. As some researchers of trauma say, a traumatic experience is not integrated into your normal sense of self. If you are traumatized, it can be the case that you think about your life, think about your personal history and there's a disruption in it—you are so shook by the traumatic experience that your memory and your ability to recall and retell what you've gone through is damaged. So is your identity and continuity through time.

So imagine that after years of torture and traumatic experiences, someone shows Brody kindness. Of course, he's in a state in which he can be easily manipulated. Brody even suspects this after finding out that Tom Walker is alive and confronts Abu Nazir about it in "Crossfire." The evil genius of Abu Nazir is that he's filled the hole that years of trauma have left in Brody's soul. In this respect, the role of Issa is also important. Issa is not only the clue that lets Carrie realize that Brody's in fact a terrorist, but the death of Issa is what gives Brody the final push and leads to the completion of his 'brainwashing'. Afterwards, Brody's convinced that he's not a terrorist, he just wants to enact revenge upon those who are responsible for the death of Issa and other school-children in the drone attack (see his confession at the beginning of "Marine One"). The torture and the traumatic experiences weakened Brody's psyche, disrupted his sense of self, which gave an opportunity to Abu Nazir to turn Brody into a terrorist. As a terrorist, Brody does not seem to be the same person as he was before. It's interesting how Abu Nazir is the only one calling Brody "Nicholas", it's as if he renamed him. Carrie sums it up: "he systematically pulled you apart, Brody . . . piece by piece until there was nothing left but pain. And then he relieved the pain and he put you back together again as someone else" ("Q&A").

Who Am I Actually Now?

Does this mean that psychological theorists are right? Well, not really. Psychological theorists of personal identity rarely pay attention to the 'sense of self' people have. A sense of self refers to something first-personal, something that the person in question has access to and can experience. Like Brody, you can probably experience if your sense of self is disrupted. Like many suffering from PTSD, Brody might feel first-personally that he is not the same person as he was. An advocate of the psychological approach could say that Brody is not the same person as he was because there is no adequate psychological continuity and connectedness between the Brody before the deployment and the Brody after. However, such an assertion is empty if we don't consider the effects of prolonged trauma on Brody's first-personal sense of self.

I can't read Brody's mind; what I can do is theorize about how his experiences affect his mind. In "The Weekend" Carrie asks Brody whether he can talk about what he's gone through with his wife, Brody replies: "It's like she doesn't know who I actually am now." She doesn't know him because he's not the same guy she used to know. We could say that Brody is conflicted: his brainwashed terrorist self is dominant, but there are traces of his old self still sort of "in there."

We haven't seen much of Brody in Season Three, but if things had turned out differently it would've been interesting to witness his Ulysses-type of homecoming to his former self just as much as it would've been exciting if he couldn't become what he used to be, no matter how hard he struggled for redemption. The events of Season Three were for Brody what electroshock therapy was for Carrie: we could be curious whether the system shock (shot, addicted, captured again) would reset him. It certainly took him to a point of suicidal indifference. In "One Last Time" Saul says to him: "I'm offering you a chance to be a marine again. The man you were before they broke you."

The Brody Carrie fell in love with, the Brody who decided that he wouldn't explode the bomb vest, the Brody who promised Dana he would come home, the Brody who's a good person, is different from the Brody who actually was "rescued." In a sense, Brody was not rescued and did not come home, not really, and in the profound sense of the word "homecoming" he wasn't able to, but he decided take a second chance and to go to war one last time.

II

Poles Apart

4
The Self-Destruction Option

JOHN V. KARAVITIS

In the first two seasons of *Homeland*, suicide is clearly presented in three separate events. The first event is the apparent suicide of one of US Marine Gunnery Sergeant Nicholas Brody's former jailers, while this person was being held in American custody. The second event is Nicholas Brody's aborted suicide bombing attempt. The third event is the successful suicide of captured al-Qaeda operative Aileen Margaret Morgan. And although many readers will disagree with me, I claim that there is a fourth suicide event.

Given the situations and motivations presented for each suicide event, is any choice to commit suicide in *Homeland* morally defensible?

No Wrong Can Be a Right

Plato (428–348 B.C.E.) felt that suicide was wrong, but that exceptions existed. Aristotle (384–322 B.C.E.) argued that suicide is not unjust as the harm that one does to oneself is consensual, but rather it is wrong insofar as it harms the community. St. Augustine (354–430) called suicide a sin, whereas St. Thomas Aquinas (1225–1274) argued that, as God gave us life, only He could determine when it would end.

In "Suicide," a short essay from his *Lectures on Ethics*, Immanuel Kant (1724–1804) reviews arguments for and against suicide. His definition of suicide is brief and to the point. "What constitutes suicide is the intention to destroy oneself." Kant also notes that the most common causes of suicide are "rage, passion, and insanity." Given this, suicide doesn't appear to be an option that would result from any moral calculus. Kant acknowledges that in fulfilling his duties, a man may find himself forced to sacrifice his life. But this would not be considered suicide. For Kant, suicide is never permissible. This final act denies your humanity, and lowers you to the level of a beast.

When All Is Lost, One Final Act

In the episode "Blind Spot" one of Abu Nazir's men, Afsal Hamid, who was also one of Nicholas Brody's former jailers, has been captured and is being held by the CIA. He isn't a soldier, so isn't accorded any rights or protections under international law, specifically the Geneva Convention. He's considered a terrorist, and it's highly unlikely that he would be given access to legal counsel or the American legal system. At best he will find himself being whisked away out of the country to a prison like the one at Guantanamo Bay, or perhaps to a prison in another country.

We see him being subjected to intense interrogation techniques—facial bruises attest to harsh beatings, sleep deprivation is presumed from loud music and bright lights, threats against his family members are plainly stated—to obtain whatever valuable intelligence he may possess about his terrorist organization. This information will be used to capture or kill his colleagues and friends, and could also indirectly put the lives of his immediate family in danger. Once he has no more information to give, he will most likely be kept in prison indefinitely. His present situation is quite bleak.

Immanuel Kant would argue that under no circumstances would suicide be morally permissible—even under these circumstances. The Stoic philosopher Lucius Annaeus Seneca (4 B.C.E.–65 C.E.), also known as Seneca the Younger, would disagree. Seneca would counsel Afsal Hamid to take his own life. In his *Moral Letters to Lucilius*, Seneca presents his ideas about how to best live your life. Stoicism urges you to focus on controlling only what you can, and to forego any desire to control what you can't.

We cannot control external events, and we all suffer misfortune of one form or another throughout our lives. However, we can control how we react to such events and misfortunes. With regard to living, Seneca sees the quality of our lives as being more important than the quantity of years we may hope to live. If your life isn't worth living, either due to a painful illness or to inescapable captivity, then there's no shame in giving up your life. Seneca's counsel to commit suicide is not capricious or whimsical; rather, it is based on a rational moral calculus. Quality of life is more important than quantity.

Suicide Is an Option

Seneca's position that suicide may be a moral act is also supported by contemporary utilitarian philosopher Peter Singer. Utilitarianism holds that you should act in such a way as to maximize the happiness or reduce the suffering of everyone involved in a decision. When faced with circumstances beyond your control, where you're imprisoned or suffering from an incurable and unbearably painful illness, it could make sense to take your own life. This euthanasia would be morally permitted because the intent would be to reduce suffering. Thus, under certain circumstances, both Stoics and utilitarians would support your right to suicide.

Brody's former jailer could assess his situation and see that all he could look forward to is at best many years of solitary confinement. If suicide would be more beneficial than continuing to live under such circumstances, all things considered, then under either Stoicism or utilitarianism, it would be morally permissible to take this final act. Here again, the right to suicide is based on a rational moral calculus. Afsal Hamid's suicide is a moral act.

The same reasoning applies to the suicide of al-Qaeda operative Aileen Margaret Morgan. In "The Clearing" Aileen has been captured and is held in solitary confinement in federal prison. After being questioned by CIA Middle East Division Chief Saul Berenson, she commits suicide, using the edge of a lens of the reading glasses that he had given her. Aileen explains why with her last words. *"I'm not going back. I'm never going back to that cave."* Again, given the circumstances, both the Stoics and the utilitarians would call her final act morally defensible.

Brody's Immoral Decision

Nicholas Brody provides the second event where suicide is presented in *Homeland*. Brody was captured in Iraq and tortured by Abu Nazir and his terrorist organization. Later he was taken to Abu Nazir's household and forced to tutor his young son in English. The death of Abu Nazir's son by an American drone strike led Brody to despise both the conflict and the American government leaders who authorized the deadly attack. Brody allows himself to be used as a suicide bomber, the targets being high-ranking American government officials.

Brody doesn't appear to be mentally ill, although you could argue that, with his conversion to Islam, he underwent Stockholm syndrome while held captive in Abu Nazir's household. He does appear to be suffering from post-traumatic stress disorder, and we know that he's being blackmailed by Abu Nazir. Brody has formally rationalized his decision to allow himself to be used as a suicide bomber as the response of a "true patriot" to the undiscovered and unpunished war crimes of his country's leaders.

Brody isn't your typical suicide bomber. Suicide bombers typically come from a civilian population whose members consider themselves oppressed by an occupying military force. When conditions change and this perception no longer exists, suicide bombers vanish. Does Brody have any moral standing to follow the path of the suicide bomber? I claim that he doesn't.

Brody was not responsible for personally addressing the illegal drone strike that killed, among others, Abu Nazir's son. His responsibility was to fully disclose the circumstances of his eight-year-long captivity to his superiors. He failed to do so. Other legitimate, moral options existed to address that terrible event. Suicide and mass murder by Brody were not defensible reactions to those circumstances. Finally, Brody's decision to go through with the suicide bombing of the high-ranking government officials was ill-thought-out and based on emotion, rationalization, and the threat of blackmail.

In "Marine One," just as he prepares to trigger his suicide vest, he gets a phone call from his teenage daughter. She pleads with him to come home. *"Dad promise me. You have to promise me that you're coming home, Dad. (sniffles) Dad? (inhales) Dad, you have to promise me. I need you. You know that."* In a nod to Aristotle, Brody's daughter is unwittingly offering the rebuttal to suicide—that everyone is needed by the community, that no one is expendable. Brody relents, and aborts the suicide mission.

If the mere pleadings of his daughter are enough to sway a man who has pledged to kill himself and many innocent others for a righteous cause, then the attempt lacks moral standing. It wasn't reasoned through thoroughly, and it has no foundation in any moral theory or calculus. Rather, Brody's decision to become a suicide bomber was based on emotions and rationalizations. Brody's decision to commit suicide, let alone commit mass murder, regardless of the reasons, and regardless of success or failure, was immoral.

Suicide by Default

There's a fourth suicide event in *Homeland*. By now you should have been wondering to whom I could have been referring, and how such an event could have gone unnoticed and unremembered by *Homeland's* viewers. We are led to believe that Brody's former jailer did in fact commit suicide (by the end of Season Two, there is no evidence to the contrary);

and we know that Aileen Morgan did commit suicide (and we know why, from her own lips). We also know that Brody was ready and willing to commit suicide and mass murder. "Who else committed suicide?" you are now asking. To this I answer that suicide need not result in the cessation of life to be a suicide.

The fourth character to experience a suicide event greets us at the beginning of every episode. She is educated, articulate, extroverted, pretty, physically fit, self-confident, driven to succeed, and patriotic. Part of what drives her is that she seeks excellence in what she does, and part is her perceived failure to predict and prevent the events of 9/11. She is Carrie Mathison, intelligence analyst for the Central Intelligence Agency. And yes, she committed suicide.

"What suicide?" you ask. In "Marine One" Carrie finally agrees to undergo electroconvulsive therapy to treat her bipolar disorder. This event constitutes a suicide because electroconvulsive therapy not only treats mental illness, it can also alter your personality by causing irreversible structural changes to your brain.

We are who we are in part because of our memories and our unique personality. Our memories are the building blocks of the narrative that makes up our lives to date. Our personality and experiences write our life's narrative from one moment to the next. Carrie's voluntary submittal to a destructive, yet necessary, medical procedure is a form of suicide. She has to destroy a part of herself in order to continue to live as a normal person. For her to live tomorrow, the person she is today must die.

Dying to Live

Carrie suffered from a mental illness, bipolar disorder, and she was secretly taking medication to control it. However, her desire to be the best, to maintain the high standards she had set for herself, and her deep-seated rage at her perceived failure to predict and prevent 9/11, drove her onward. It also resulted in alienating her coworkers, her friends, and her family. To her credit, Carrie strove for excellence, but she did so at too high a cost.

In the spectrum from commitment to obsession, Carrie ran headlong into the latter. Her rage at her failure to at least anticipate the possibility of the events of 9/11 drove her into a refusal to heed the warnings of her family, friends, and coworkers. Her refusal to openly address and treat her mental illness, which would have resulted in her dismissal from the CIA, led to her rage eventually turning against herself. Her negligence at not living a balanced life led to her eventual decision to undergo electroconvulsive therapy, and this was a form of suicide. To live, the old Carrie had to die.

If you're willing to accept my argument, then you may find yourself feeling that Carrie's actions thus have moral standing. If letting her old self go would allow her to have a new lease on life, how could this not be moral? In fact, Carrie's decision to undergo electroconvulsive therapy was neither moral nor immoral. Her decision to submit to electroconvulsive therapy was the end result of her persistent refusal to put her health ahead of her career, and her persistent refusal to come to terms with her rage.

Her rage, along with her perfectionist demands in her career, were personal failings that finally drove her to electroconvulsive therapy. The "euthanasia" was not so much voluntary as it was the result of personal negligence. Carrie did not fully work out the consequences of her decision. She had forced her attention away from herself, away from living a balanced life, and she ended up destroying who she was. Her suicide was not moral. It did not result from a reasoned consideration under a moral theory or framework. On the other hand, her suicide was not immoral. It was not made on a whim, nor in the heat of the moment, nor could she have been easily swayed from her decision. Rather, Carrie's suicide was amoral.

Contemporary philosopher Peter Sloterdijk, writing in *Rage and Time*, would have understood Carrie's predicament perfectly. "This turn against oneself can come about when a person does not live up to the expectations that would have to be satisfied in order for that person not to lose self-respect," claims Sloterdijk. Carrie's rage and unrealistic demands on herself meant that help was accepted only when there was no other choice. Carrie strove for excellence at too high a cost, and the suicide of her old self was inevitable. Being inevitable; neither reasoned out thoroughly, nor taken on a caprice or whim; and taken without seeking out other options or opportunities, all make her suicide amoral.

Look Deep into the Mirror

All four of the suicide events in Homeland can be seen as being the end results of rage, a rage that began as a kernel which blossomed into a final act of despair.

Brody's former jailer was possessed by his rage at the perceived injustices perpetrated by invading American forces. It drove him to join a terrorist organization, which only made life worse for many innocent people.

Aileen Morgan's rage at the perceived injustice of American military actions led her to become a low-level al-Qaeda operative. Once captured, she understood that her life was over, and her rage turned to despair.

Brody's rage resulted from the death of Abu Nazir's son by an unjustified, illegal American drone strike. It drove him to allow himself to become a willing pawn in the planned mass murder of people who had done neither him nor his family any harm.

Carrie's rage resulted from her high standards, her blind search for excellence at too high a cost, and her sense of failure at not predicting the events of 9/11. Her rage, like the rage of Achilles, eventually led to the loss of her own self. True, rage is an emotion, and emotions help us decide what to turn our attention to. But rage is an emotion that can lead one to make rash decisions that lead to irreversible consequences.

Suicide is a serious act. It means that the suicide has given up any possibility of any other course of action that would include continuing to live. It denies one's future self the chance to live. If the decision is based on a moral framework or theory, and is rationally arrived at, then one should proceed confidently from one's judgment, even if everyone else, under the same circumstances, would have chosen differently. Many philosophers would support this final act as a moral act. An unfortunate act, but a moral one nevertheless.

If the suicide is based on emotional considerations, rationalizations, and ignores possible alternatives that would allow the individual to continue to live, then the suicide lacks moral standing. It is immoral. If one lives one's life destructively, and out-of-balance, a suicide of sorts can occur, but it is neither based on a moral framework, nor is it based on caprice or whim. Such a suicide can only be amoral.

Let's learn from the misfortunes of the characters in *Homeland*, and learn to look deep, deep inside. Life is worth living, and is short enough as it is. The end will come—eventually. It will for all of us. And as you can't tell what the future will bring—anything can happen—you should give your future self a chance at life.

Don't be so eager to let go.

5
Broken Love in *Homeland*

BRITTANY LORENZ AND ADAM BARKMAN

In the pilot episode of *Homeland,* the first scene opens with a pan view of Baghdad. We hear the voice of Carrie Mathison and later see her. From the first few minutes of the show, the viewer is drawn into the world of the CIA. The tension, the intensity, and the demanding nature of national security are portrayed in the initial scenes of the pilot.

Throughout the first three seasons of the show, the viewer encounters a bevy of characters, each with a distinct and important role in the plot. The way that all the characters fit together creates an incredibly tangled web, and at the heart of this web is not "terrorism," or "the CIA," or "freedom," but love and its brokenness.

Through the relationships between Brody and Jessica, Mira and Saul, Carrie and Brody and Brody and his family, *Homeland* presents the viewer with a broken view of love. Indeed, the show is an excellent landscape upon which the viewer can spot notions of love mentioned in two important works about love: C.S. Lewis's *The Four Loves* and Aristotle's *Nicomachean Ethics*.

Look Me in the Eye and Tell Me You Felt Nothing Up in That Cabin

I (Brittany) remember being eight years old and sitting with my friends at recess, talking about boys. The recurring question was: Do you "like" him or "like, like" him—as if saying the word twice with a different tone of voice made it mean something entirely different. The fact was it did. My childhood experience suggests a larger problem with our English language. No one would expect that at the age of eight, I would or could say I "loved" this boy I went to school with. Yet everyone seems to recognize that their "love" for pizza is different from the "love" they have for a pet, and that both of these are different types of love than that which they have for their children or spouse. English has just one word for all these different kinds of love, so the term "love" gets used to describe many kinds of relationships.

To better identify the different types of love that we are talking about we must turn to the Greek language, which has four different terms for what the English language call love: *storgé, eros, philia,* and *agapé*. Each represents a different yet crucial aspect of our understanding of love as used in different types of relationships. One who loves perfectly would be said to embody each of these kinds of love in a relationship.

Saul . . . We're Like Good Friends Sharing a House

Storgé is said to be the most basic of the loves and can be enjoyed by anyone with sentience (even lower animals). It is roughly defined as affection developed upon the basis of familiarity. Storgé is a very uncomplicated feeling. Storgé can be felt for your country, a tree in your yard, a brand of potato chips, your wife, a marketplace, or a stranger. The key to understanding storgé as a love is that it is based on proximity and closeness—the object of this love must be familiar. Because you are close to something either accidently or on purpose you are going to feel some familiarity with it given enough time. In relationships, storgé is experienced between any persons who spend time together regardless of whether we would define this time spent as "quality time" or if it is simply two people who ride the same subway every morning to work.

In *Homeland* we see terrorism as the brokenness of one type of love: storgé. Terrorism is a brokenness of storgé because it *doesn't allow you to be comfortable anymore*. It threatens the comfort or the ease, and creates instability. When terrorism is present, you can no longer feel comfortable with a certain thing such as a familiar place like your home or market. In *Homeland* we see terrorism as a threat against The United States; the whole fight for national security is for safety but also to restore storgé for the nation— to restore a feeling of ease, comfort, and stability. Even the most familiar of places can make you feel uneasy because you fear that at any point there could be a suicide bomb, or a drone strike. Terrorism doesn't allow storgé to flourish because familiarity can't be developed when citizens are living in fear. Terrorism threatens the comfort of the people who live in a country; they no longer feel safe or secure and it is in this that *Homeland* shows the brokenness of storgé.

I Want You to Leave Your Wife and Children and Be with Me

The second kind of love we see in *Homeland* is *eros*, which is attraction, especially sexual attraction, and the feeling of "being in love." Proper eros, that is, when eros is functioning well, is monogamously inclined—it wants "this one" and only "this one." Thus when "being in love" is functioning properly, it is a passionate dedication to the one love. Eros sees the object of its desire and loves it despite its flaws—one might be tempted to call it blind, yet in another, important sense, it exercises greater clarity than any other type of love since it sees divinity—the soul—of the person and not just its animal nature. This is all in Plato and the Bible.

An example of well-functioning eros is shown in the episode "The Weekend," where Saul is talking to Aileen, a low-level al-Qaeda operative whom Saul has arrested in Mexico:

AILEEN: So, what's the trouble at home?

SAUL: Nothing much. Just the love of my life walking out my door.

AILEEN: For good?

SAUL: I hope not. 'Cause I can't imagine being that lost.

Although we later find out that Saul's wife has been with another man, we recognize eros to be properly functioning when it comes to Saul and his love for his wife Mira since he sees Mira, and only Mira, and desires her above all others, despite the flaws and the hardships. But this is perhaps the only example of properly functioning eros in the show.

Throughout the first three seasons of *Homeland* we see a strange "love square" develop between Brody and Jessica, who are married; Mike who was having an affair with Jessica; and Carrie, who had an affair with Brody. There is no better example of broken eros than to look at the way that these four characters interact and the relationships between them. Perverse eros does not desire the beloved him or herself, but only the pleasures that can be obtained from the other. Broken eros desires the sexual pleasures that the other can give and that's that. What is desired is the sex and the feeling, not the beloved themselves. We see an excellent example of this in respect to Mira in "A Red Wheelbarrow":

MIRA'S LOVER: I love you.

MIRA: Don't say that.

MIRA'S LOVER: I love making love to you.

This quote embodies our understanding of broken eros. Mira seems to have knowledge of how the relationship with her lover is not true eros, but seeking the feeling and sexual pleasure the other can provide rather than the person themselves. In respect to our "love square," we also see this with Carrie and Brody in "I'll Fly Away":

CARRIE: I don't want you to feel used.

BRODY: I do feel used. . . . I also feel good. Two minutes with you and I feel good.

Brody, who is married, desires Carrie simply for the good feeling that she can provide.

According to Sherif Girgis and colleagues in their book *What Is Marriage?* (2012), marriage is designed to be a

comprehensive union: joining spouses in body as well as in mind; it is begun by consent and sealed by coitus. . . . It also calls for an all-encompassing commitment: permanent and exclusive.

If we assume this conjugal view of marriage or natural marriage and believe that a properly functioning marriage is erotically monogamous, then we would view Brody's and Jessica's marriage as broken. The fact that we see infidelity in their marriage reflects the brokenness of eros. Jessica doesn't desire Brody over any other nor does Brody, Jessica. Both have by consent established this marriage and it has been sealed with sexual intercourse thus meaning that it should be permanent and exclusive. The lack of permanence and exclusivity in their marriage shows a brokenness of erotic justice or justice in respect to eros since neither participant is treating the other as the sole participants in the marriage, as such.

Is This for Real? Are You Just Handling Me?

The third type of love that we see in *Homeland* is *philia* or friendship, which is perhaps the least understood of the loves in our day and age. This type of love is based on rationality and common interests, meaning, among other things, that mere time spent together (storgé) is not enough to establish philia. It is our common loves that unite us as friends. If two rational beings share no love of a common object, then there can be no philia. Two people can experience philia on the basis of a common interest in a TV show, but if they do not share the same worldview this friendship will always be a bit thin.

We see something like this in Brody's and Jessica's marriage. When Brody returns from his eight years in captivity, he has converted to Islam. Instead of coming out and telling his wife that he has taken on this faith, he hides it from her, thus not allowing his most basic and important beliefs to be known, much less shared, with his wife. This puts a serious damper on their philia.

It isn't until the premiere of Season Two that Jessica finds out that Brody is a Muslim (after Dana says that her father is a Muslim during an argument at school which resulted in the dean calling Jessica about the incident). Brody himself eventually tells Jessica that he is a Muslim, which results in a rage-filled Jessica storming to the garage where Brody tells her that he prays. After throwing Brody's copy of the Quran on the garage floor her response to all of this in the Season Two premiere is:

> I thought you put this crazy stuff behind you. . . . This can't happen, you have a wife, two kids, you're a congressman in the running to be Vice President. It cannot happen. You get that, right?

Brody didn't want to tell Jessica because he knew it would upset her, but in keeping his religion from her there was no foundation upon which a strong *philia* could grow.

The other way that we see friendships—broken friendships—portrayed in *Homeland* is through utility, where some friendships are used simply or primarily as a means to gain power. Many characters in *Homeland* are turned into double agents; we see this with Brody, whose allegiance is turned and he uses his friendships that have previously been established to gain information to use against people. To a certain extent, this might not be so much "broken" as "imperfect," but still; not ideal. Why? Aristotle wrote about three different types of friendships in *Nicomachean Ethics*, one of which is friendship of utility. Aristotle describes friendships of utility in this way: "Those who are friends on account of utility dissolve the friendship at the same time as the advantage ceases, for they were friends not of each other but to the profit involved."

This type of friendship—which few us nowadays would even be willing to call a friendship in any meaningful sense—is not Aristotle's ideal friendship, which is a rational relation surrounding common interests and based on genuine concern for the other as such: "Now those who love each other for their utility do not love each other for themselves but in virtue of some good which they get from each other." The basis for philia is common loves and interests and friendship of utility do not create this foundation upon which proper or ideal philia can be built.

We see a specific instance of a friendship of utility between Abu Nazir and Brody. Abu Nazir uses Brody in order to achieve vengeance on the soul of Issa, his deceased son who was killed in a drone strike ordered by the Vice President of the United States. Nazir tries to use his relationship with Brody as a means to an end. There is no proper or ideal philia; rather we see that to the other each becomes merely an opportunity for benefit, reflecting a brokenness of the love philia.

The Dots Are There, Carrie, but You Haven't Connected Them Yet

The final love that we see in *Homeland* is *agapé* or sacrificial love. Agapé has two specific conditions inherent to it. The first is that in order for agapé to be proper and praiseworthy, it must never violate or contradict justice. And the second is that it must go beyond the requirements of justice. Agapé goes beyond the requirement of justice without contradicting it, which makes it the supreme ethical mode. To clarify, let's consider Brody's relation to his country.

To love one's country is to feel storgé for it, and for me to feel this love is proper and just. That is, if I were to feel no sense of patriotism, and have any sense of moral obligation derived from this sense of patriotism, I would be truly unnatural, both in terms of having improperly functioning affections and in terms of reasoning badly about my derived moral obligations. Yet all this said, my storgé for my country doesn't absolutely require me to go overseas and die for my country.

In the case of Brody, we could argue that his sense of, and actions derived from, agapé are broken. Certainly, Brody goes overseas to Iraq to fight in a war against terrorism abroad, and in some situations this could be construed as agapé, but not always—not even often.

As a father and a husband Brody's first obligations are to his wife and children. If he can satisfy his duties to his family by going abroad and fighting for his country, then we might be able to see this as justice being perfected with agapé. For example, if there were a clear and imminent threat to his family by Muslim extremists—instead of a more distant, ideological threat—then we could say that protecting his family from an imminent threat would be just and his act of risking his life, proper agapé. But in the case of Brody, he is violating justice by going abroad because there are obligations that are not met as a result of him going to fight on behalf of his country. He isn't directly fulfilling his obligations as a husband and father, to be a husband to his wife and to raise his son and daughter. In order for his actions to become heroic and praiseworthy, agapé would have to be done through justice ensuring that all his first duties are met; yet because they are not, agapé is another broken love in *Homeland*.

A Window to Redemption?

Throughout *Homeland* we are presented with many types of love: storgé, eros, philia and agapé. More to the point, we can find examples of all these types of loves broken—through terrorism, infidelity, friendships of utility, and duties abandoned in the name of patriotism.

We see and feel the effects of broken love throughout the show and the pain is palpable. Yet the viewer finds himself or herself holding onto the few glimpses of properly functioning love in the show as a means of hope for the future. Indeed, it is with these glimpses in mind that we see a small window into how these various loves might look if they were ever to be mended, restored, or redeemed.

III

Land of the Free

6
Brainwashed Brody's Freedom

DAN BURKETT

In the Season One episode "Marine One" Sergeant Brody dons a suicide vest while locked in a bunker with the men responsible for Issa's death. Brody chooses to flip the detonator switch, but is he a bad person for doing this?

We usually take someone's moral responsibility for an action to be closely tied to how *free* that person was when he or she acted. We are more likely to forgive someone who is *forced* into doing something bad than someone who chose to do it freely. How does this help Brody? Suppose we took on the job of defending him against the claim that he's a morally bad person for flipping that switch.

One way we could do this is by arguing that he *wasn't acting freely* when he did it. His relationship with Issa was carefully fostered by Abu Nazir, and came at a time when Brody had already undergone months of torture, isolation, and deprivation. He was—to all intents and purposes—brainwashed, and for this reason, should not be held morally responsible for his actions while in that bunker.

Two Kinds of Freedom

The concept of "freedom" is difficult to pin down—especially since there's little consensus on what this term actually means. One view is that a person is "free" when their actions

57

match up with what they desire. Consider, for example, the difference between a man who starves himself in order to protest against the war in Afghanistan, and a man who starves because he is stranded in the desert without any food. The former, it seems, starves *freely*. Not eating is exactly what he desires to do. The latter, however, does *not* starve freely. His starvation is forced upon him by his circumstances.

This view of freedom certainly seems plausible. Suppose we apply it to one of Brody's questionable actions—his apparent murder of Corporal Thomas Walker. In the Season One episode "The Weekend", Brody confesses to Carrie that he is the one responsible for Walker's death. He explains, however, that he was forced to do this terrible thing:

> I killed him. They told me to beat him to death or be killed myself. . . . And so I did it.

In this case, Brody was subjected to an incredibly strong case of coercion. He was given an option between Walker's life and his own. It seems that prior to this threat Brody had no desire whatsoever to see Walker dead, let alone be the one to kill him.

We might say that after the threat was made, Brody did— in some sense—desire Walker's death: that is, *he desired Walker's death as the only means of saving his (Brody's) own life*. If he didn't, then he never would have gone through with killing Walker. But is this fair to Brody? In a situation in which his choices were so limited—not to mention unthinkable—does it make sense to say that he genuinely "desired" the option he chose? Suppose that Brody had been scheduled for torture the previous morning, but was generously given the option between either being waterboarded or whipped. After some consideration Brody chose the latter, but would it really make sense to say that he *desired* to be whipped?

Our answer will most likely be "no." So long as we hold this position, we should also deny that Brody "desired" to kill Walker in any meaningful sense of the word. If this is true, then—on the definition of freedom given above—Brody *was not free in killing Walker*, and therefore not morally responsible for this action.

For many people, this conclusion will be no surprise. It seems that a man in Brody's horrible circumstances (that is, a man forced to choose between his own life, and the life of another) will be treated far less harshly than a man who kills because he actually wishes to see someone dead. But the unsurprising nature of this answer is a good thing. It means that the theory of freedom we're talking about (and the idea that a *lack* of freedom seems to lead to a *lack* of moral responsibility) matches with our intuitions—with the way we naturally tend to think. We might say many things about Brody's action—that it was cowardly, or dishonorable, or that a "real soldier" would have sacrificed himself to save his comrade's life—but this is a long way from saying that it was *morally wrong*.

But is this kind of freedom *strong* enough? The philosopher John Locke didn't think so, and posed an ingenious thought experiment to show this. We can consider a variation of it now: Suppose that after seeing Carrie's deteriorating mental state, her sister Maggie decides to lock Carrie inside her own home one night in order to keep her safe. Carrie is completely unaware of this. She imagines herself to be free to leave at any time, even though—were she to try—she would be unable to do so. Fortunately, Carrie is perfectly content there. She has wine, and yogurt, and enough classified CIA documents to construct hundreds of complex timelines on her living room walls. She is exactly where she most desires to be. It seems, then, that Carrie freely stays home that night.

But is this right? Does this seem like a genuine case of freedom? For Locke and many others, this way of thinking simply doesn't give the right answer in this case. It's from this observation that we get our second—and much stronger—definition of freedom, usually referred to as "libertarianism" (though this is a different kind of "libertarianism" to the one usually found in political discussion).

According to libertarianism, an action will only be free if it matches our desires *and we could have done otherwise in the circumstances*. While Carrie may desire to stay home that night, she was entirely unable to do anything else. This means that on the libertarian view Carrie doesn't stay home freely. In order to have done this, Carrie must have been able to do otherwise—that is, to leave her home.

Did Brody Freely Flip the Switch?

By the time Brody finds himself in that bunker, he's been through a lot. During his captivity he was beaten, tortured, and subjected to long periods of total isolation. After his body was broken, his captors went to work on his mind—forcing him to apparently kill his comrade. Finally, after all of this, Abu Nazir came to Brody and presented himself as a savior, inspiring a feverish loyalty and adoration. Brody says as much of Nazir in "The Weekend":

> He offered me comfort . . . And I took it . . . I was broken, living in the dark for years. And a man walked in. And he was kind to me. And I loved him.

The manipulation didn't stop there however. Brody was soon introduced to Nazir's son, Issa, and ordered to teach the boy English. Over the ensuing months Brody and Issa developed a deep friendship, with Issa serving as something of a substitute for Brody's own far-away children. There's no doubt that Issa's death in the drone strike was the catalyst for Brody's turn. In the Season One episode "Crossfire", Nazir says to Brody that he prays every day that "you never lose sight of what you committed to do *in Issa's name*". In fact, the final words Brody hears in his head before flipping the detonator switch are not those of his wife or children, but of Nazir simply saying "Remember Issa . . ."

Given all of this, can we really say that Brody is *acting freely* when he flips that switch? Does it not seem to be the case that after *years* of physical and mental torture—not to mention subtle and insidious psychological manipulation—his actions are no longer his own? He is programmed. Brainwashed. A slave to the commands of Nazir. It's a bold claim—and one that may be difficult to defend. But it's really the only argument we can make if we have any hope of proving that Brody is not morally responsible for this terrible action.

Consider, first, whether or not Brody is free in the first sense we looked at. Unlike his "murder" of Walker, there is no immediate threat looming over Brody's head. He is not being told to carry out the attack "or else". It seems that, despite understandable anxiety and trepidation (he is, after all, preparing to commit suicide), Brody very much desires to detonate the bomb. He is there to avenge Issa. To make those responsible for the drone strike *pay* for what they did. If this is true, then Brody is very much free in flipping the switch.

The question of whether or not Brody is free in the second sense—the libertarian sense—is far more difficult to answer. Suppose that Brody's experiences over the previous eight years did amount to an incredibly intricate and complete case of brainwashing. Would this be enough to say that—despite his desires—he is still unfree? In that final moment when his finger is resting on the switch, can we really say that Brody is unable to do otherwise—that he had an absolute inability to refrain from triggering the detonator? Unfortunately, a number of factors work against us in making this argument.

In "Crossfire" Nazir clearly states to Brody that "it was *your choice* doing what you are doing", seemingly affirming that Brody is acting freely. But, of course, Nazir *would* say that. The greatest deception of all in these cases is to convince an individual that they are acting freely when in reality they completely lack any ability to do otherwise (consider again the case of Carrie being locked in her home). Suppose Nazir is telling the truth, and Brody did in fact choose to carry out the attack. This will count for nothing if it turns out that—given his brainwashing—*this was the only choice that Brody could have made*. In order for Brody to have chosen freely, it must have been the case that he had a number of choices open to him, any of which he could have selected.

Prior to his bombing attempt, Brody films a confession video in which he provides a reply to the very argument we are trying to make here. He acknowledges the fact that "people will say I was broken. *I was brainwashed.* People will say that I was turned into a terrorist." He goes on to deny that this is what has actually happened. Here, we're attempting to defend Brody by arguing that he was not morally responsible because he was not free. Brody, on the other hand, is dead set on showing us that this is not true.

But can we even take Brody at his word? If an individual can be programmed to kill—and to sacrifice himself and cause irreparable harm to those he loves most—then surely he can be programmed to insist that he acted freely in doing all of this? If Brody truly *is* brainwashed, we can pay no attention to the justifications he gives either for his actions or for why he was free in doing them.

Our best chance of defending Brody—of holding that he was not, in fact, morally responsible for triggering the detonator—is this: to adopt the libertarian view of freedom and argue that (despite his protestations to the contrary) his experiences while in captivity led him to a state where he was completely unable to do otherwise by the time he finds himself in that bunker. If this is the case, then we can't hold him responsible for his actions. Sergeant Nicholas Brody is not morally responsible for flipping the switch.

Destined to Fail

Free or not, Brody ultimately flips the switch. Fortunately, however, the vest malfunctions and fails to detonate. This fault in Brody's equipment means that his attack was always determined to fail, regardless of his intentions. Suppose that our argument from above fails and that Brody *should* be held responsible for flipping the switch. Does the inevitability of the vest's failure leave Brody in a better moral position than if the vest had functioned as intended?

Our answer to this question turns on how we choose to judge the moral value of actions. One position we might take is known as consequentialism, according to which the moral value of an action is determined by its consequences. The situation in which the bomb malfunctions certainly seems better than the situation in which it works as intended. Consequentialism will agree with this, so long as we assume that the deaths of the people in the bunker would actually be a bad thing. But should this lead us to say that Brody is a morally better person just because the vest failed to work? That certainly seems an unusual claim to make. Brody's intentions are the same, whether the vest works or not. He means to kill every person in that room. The fact that he fails to do this comes down to a matter of mere *luck* (bad luck for his plan, but good luck for his intended victims).

If we have a problem with judging Brody's action by its actual outcome, then it seems that it's more than just consequences that matter. The intentions of the person also play an important role. While there's a clear difference between a case where the vest works, and a case where it doesn't, Brody (assuming he's free) still seems to have done something *morally wrong* in both cases. He *intends* for the bomb to detonate, killing everyone within its blast radius. A small defect in the wiring of the vest is not enough to make him morally unblameworthy.

Sergeant Brody's Redemption?

Brody manages to repair the malfunctioning vest, and sets himself up for a second attempt. He's interrupted, however, by a call from his daughter, Dana. Sensing something is wrong, and rattled by her encounter with Carrie, Dana pleads with her father to return home.

> You have to promise me that you're coming home. . . . Dad, you have to promise me. *I need you.* You know that.

After a few agonizing moments of indecision, Brody finally replies: "I'm coming home, Dana. I promise." In that moment, he decides to abandon the attack. Is this the redemption of Sergeant Nicholas Brody? Has he finally *done the morally right thing*?

Our answer to this question depends on the answer to our earlier question—was Brody morally responsible for flipping the switch in the first place? In many ways, Dana's words do just as much to affect Brody's freedom as Nazir's brainwashing. She appeals to her father's paternal instinct and enormous devotion to his children. She asks him something that no loving father could deny—to come home to her, and to care for her. Dana's intentions are far more pure than Nazir's. All she wants is her father—a reasonable demand of any frightened and concerned child. Nazir's brainwashing of Brody, on the other hand, was merely a case of malicious manipulation. Nevertheless, we might argue that by making this phone call, Dana restricts Brody's ability to do otherwise in the very same way that Nazir did. After Dana's call Brody is overcome, overwhelmed, and left with an inability to do anything other than abandon the attack, exit the bunker, and head home to his family.

What this similarity means, however, is that if Brody was not responsible for his morally *wrong* action of pressing the button, he is also not responsible for his later morally *right* action of abandoning the attack. This is a problem. We don't want to blame him for flipping the switch, but we do want to applaud him for abandoning the attack. Unfortunately, we cannot have our cake and eat it too. If he is not responsible for one, then he is not responsible for the other.

Perhaps the best way to defend Brody is to abandon all attempts to say that his freedom was ever in question. We should admit that when he flipped that switch, he not only desired to do so, *but also could have done otherwise*. Despite the years of torture and manipulation, he could have refrained from detonating the vest, and for this reason he was entirely morally responsible for this heinous act. The vest may have failed, but—as we've seen—this does nothing to absolve him of his action. He intended to take a large number of lives, and ruin even more.

How exactly does this help our case for Brody? Well, this concession allows us to make a far more powerful claim: that is, that when his daughter rings him—when he hears her pleas and is reminded of what truly matters to him—he calls off the attack, *and he does so freely*. He does the morally right thing and walks away, proving that he remains, at heart, a good man.

6
The Illusion of Freedom

APRIL MARRATTO AND ADAM BARKMAN

Human beings are not, nor should they be, free. We are obsessed with the notion of freedom in the West. We idolize freedom and become unglued at the slightest hint that someone is infringing upon our freedom. This infatuation with freedom is, however, a paradox because the reality is that we are not truly free beings.

It is, of course, paramount to this discussion to define freedom. For the purpose of our discussion, therefore, we will define freedom—political freedom specifically—with these two senses in mind: the right to speak, act, and think however one desires, and the state of neither being enslaved nor imprisoned. In both senses, most citizens of western nations would be considered free creatures. More specifically, the American characters in *Homeland*—Brody, his family, Carrie, Saul, and a few others—appear to be so free. But are they so free? And should they be so free?

Are We Free?

One of philosopher Michel Foucault's major attacks on the concept of freedom comes from his co-opting of Jeremy Bentham's panopticon. In the late eighteenth century, Bentham designed a penitentiary system, called the *panopticon*. (It was never implemented.) In the panopticon, there is a watchman in a tower at the center of a circular structure. All of the cells of the inmates face the center so that the watchman can observe and monitor them; however, the important feature is that the inmates cannot see the person in the watchtower. This way it is possible to remove the watchman, and the inmates would never know whether he was there or not; they would be living under the fear that their every move was being scrutinized.

Foucault takes this concept and appropriates it for society as a whole in his book *Discipline and Punish*. Foucault writes, "the Panopticon must not be understood as a dream building: it is the diagram of a mechanism of power reduced to its ideal form . . . and must be detached from any specific use." In other words, the threat of surveillance is enough to keep the power structure in place.

Of course, in *Homeland* the threat of surveillance isn't just an idle threat; right away in the pilot episode Brody is placed under illegal surveillance by Carrie, a CIA agent who thinks he may be a terrorist. Carrie has a gut feeling that Brody is a terrorist based on information given to her by a dying informant. This gut feeling then leads to her watching his home; thus, not only is Brody under surveillance, but his entire family loses their freedom *without knowing it*. It is important to say that Carrie was right about Brody, but when the surveillance was first set up, she had no proof; further, in the episode "Grace," Saul, her boss, is able to find a judge to make the surveillance legal, meaning that, based on Carrie's hunch and illegally obtained information, the CIA was able to legally spy on a house of American citizens.

Remember the first sense of our definition of freedom—the ability to think, act, and speak however we wish? Brody and his family, through the surveillance, lose a significant chunk of this dimension of freedom. Their actions are being watched and documented, potentially to be used against them, should Brody be found guilty. Their words are being listened to—they have no privacy. All of their interactions as a family, even the kind of tea Brody drinks, or the couple's attempts to renew the sexual component of their marriage are being watched and studied.

Homeland taps into the idea that we can be subjects of surveillance at any time by showing us a family whose freedoms are taken away before a real threat is discovered—they are guilty until proven innocent; their freedom has been restricted before substantial evidence has been gathered. Foucault's warning seems apt here: we can see Brody and his family living imprisoned in this sense, and we the viewers recognize that we could also be.

Body's daughter, Dana, is the character who appears most aware of her loss of freedom. Throughout the show she experiences various impediments to her personal freedom. In the episode "The Smile," Dana is trying to figure out how to behave in her new school, with a new crowd of people. The school is having a discussion time and the topic turns to religion. Dana, having recently discovered that her father has converted to Islam, blurts out that her father is a Muslim. Another student in the school quickly turns the announcement into a joke, but it is made clear that it is not appropriate for Brody to be a Muslim, especially since he is now a congressman. Brody's wife, Jessica, emphasizes this when she finds out about the incident later. Dana quickly realizes that the freedom to think, act, and speak does not exist to the degree to which she had previously thought, or it exists largely to the degree to which one obeys a certain social-political code.

An Illusion?

Foucault believes that our freedom is an illusion—that there are power structures at play in the world and that we are always subject to those in power over us. A great example of this concept is the episode "Two Hats," in which Brody's family is taken to a safe house because he has revealed secrets about terrorist Abu Nazir. No one in the family has any idea why they are going to a safe house, and none of them is able to leave freely. Dana, again, feels this the most strongly; she wants to go to school; she wants to be able to do as she wishes, and feels frustrated by the loss of her freedom.

Foucault would suggest that this episode points to the idea that a person's freedom is limited and can be taken away at any time. While we may interject that it's with good reason that our freedom can be suspended (more on this later), this doesn't alter the fact that Brody's family, people who personally have done nothing to warrant a removal of their freedoms, can't act, think, or speak as they wish, and now have been, in effect, imprisoned.

Homeland does a remarkable job of presenting this loss of freedom in such a way that we, as the audience, do not on the whole lament their loss of freedom. We get it. Brody tried to become a suicide bomber, and his family is in danger. After 9/11, we may even understand, even if we disagree, why, as a congressman, being a Muslim may present certain difficulties. So, while we can acknowledge that freedoms appear to be taken away, we certainly sympathize with the reasons for it. In this way, *Homeland* forces us to change the question. Foucault shows us that potentially our freedom is illusory in that it is subject to those in power, but the new question *Homeland* brings to the table is: Should we really be free?

Should We Be Free?

Foucault's entire premise rests on the concept that we *should* be free in the sense of freedom we've been using throughout. If we can determine that absolute, unrestricted political freedom isn't a worthy goal, than it matters little if our freedom is illusory. Do we really believe that a suspected terrorist deserves to be free to think, act, and speak in any way he pleases? Perhaps not; when it comes to protecting the greater good, some individual freedoms can be trumped by a commitment to the greater good.

In "One Last Time" Brody is brought back to the United States by Saul. Brody fled because he was implicated in a bombing that killed many CIA agents, although by this time it appears as though Brody is innocent. In the past, Brody had fully co-operated with Saul and the CIA as retribution for his crimes, but this bombing returned him to enemy status. Saul realized that since Brody has been blamed for the bomb internationally that Brody would make a very good informant; however, when he finds Brody, in the episode "The Red Wheelbarrow," Brody is a despondent heroin addict. Upon his arrival back in the States, Brody quickly undergoes a forced detox; Saul is determined to have Brody ready to be sent to Iran to be the high level informant Saul requires for his CIA operation.

At this point, Saul does not believe Brody is guilty of setting the bomb that destroyed the CIA, and Brody has confessed to, and paid for, his past offences. While Brody was on the run a family died trying to protect him, but that is irrelevant to his debt to the United States. Saul's desire to use these situations to persuade Brody into agreeing to the detox appears utilitarian. Saul needs Brody to act as an informant so that Saul can infiltrate a large terrorist organization in an effort to protect the American population. In other words, Brody is forced to give up his freedom and undergo a painfully fast detox for the sake of the general American populace.

We've already suggested that Foucault would argue that this treatment of Brody further emphasizes the point that we are not really free as individuals. It's time to turn our attention to two other philosophers: Aristotle and Jean-Jacques Rousseau.

Aristotelian Self-Direction

Since Aristotle did give specific guidelines for slaves, some accuse him of being opposed to personal freedom, but that is a bit of a misreading. Aristotle is responding to the people of his time and how they treated their slaves; he was not an enthusiastic advocate of slavery. In his book, *Politics*, Aristotle outlines the nature of freedom, and how freedom should work in society at large. For Aristotle, it was the ability to have a self-directed will that defined freedom, rather than being able to simply act however we pleased. Aristotle held a notion of virtue—choosing rightly—and believed that education is important for this. Having a self-directed will is about being able to choose rightly for yourself, not about being able to act however one wants.

In the episode "I'll Fly Away," Dana, having been a passenger in a hit and run, realized that it is proper to go and make things right with the family she has wronged. Despite attempts to thwart her desire, she does eventually visit the daughter of the woman killed in the accident. While the meeting does not go as planned, Dana was able to use her freedom to exercise right virtue, and in that way, Aristotle would maintain she has kept her freedom.

Aristotle thought that your personal freedom must be kept in check by your responsibility to the city-state. So, our personal political freedom is subject to the country, state, or city in which we reside. Here we give up a significant measure of our personal, political freedom for the sake of the greater good. Aristotle would probably have supported Saul's decision to force Brody into a painful detox if it meant the protection of the country. For Aristotle, it is rational that one person's freedom should not be protected at the expense of the potential lives of many people. Which raises the question: who gets to decide when someone should lose some of their freedom?

Rousseau and Overthrow

In the sixteenth century, Rousseau composed the *Social Contract*, a treatise regarding the best way to establish a political community. A major aspect of this book is the idea of authority or the question of who gets to decide what is better for the greater good of the state.

Rousseau's concept includes the idea of a sovereign, which is irrelevant in our context. His concept of government, however, is very relevant. Basically, he believes that through citizenship we enter into a social contract in which we agree to behave in a way that is deemed acceptable to the government. Rousseau maintains freedom by suggesting that each person relinquishes the same amount of rights, while at the same time assuming the same amount of duties. The government is meant to enact the laws given by the people, like in a democracy, and if they overstep, Rousseau believes the people should overthrow the government and choose another one. So the people and the government work together to establish an idea of authority. There is a sense of balance; no one person has more authority than anyone else. The people would keep the government in check, and likewise the government would ensure that the people are following the social contract.

This means that in a particular situation like Brody's detox, the government would get to make the decision whether Brody should relinquish his personal rights. Rousseau, himself, believed that larger countries had a harder time protecting the freedom of their citizens because in larger countries, governments required stronger control over their citizens. So, it would make sense, for Rousseau, that an American runs a greater risk of losing their personal freedom for the sake of the country. In this way, Rousseau would, like Aristotle, likely side with Saul in believing that Brody should undergo the detox, even if it requires the removal of his personal freedom.

Aristotle and Rousseau, too, would agree that sending Brody's family to a safe house is appropriate, for Aristotle, it would be because the protection of the family is of utmost importance, and for Rousseau, he would believe that the government has a right to protect women and children. Neither philosopher would see this example as a direct loss of freedom. Aristotle would believe that Brody's family is not inhibited from choosing rightly by being forced into the safe house; therefore, their ability to have a self-directed will is not hampered. Rousseau, on the other hand, would see the participation in the social contract as a choice. If Brody's family is reaping the benefits of being American citizens, then they should also find it acceptable to relinquish certain rights when it is deemed necessary. In this way, Aristotle and Rousseau would oppose Foucault in his belief that freedom is an absolute, and that any infringement on freedom is an infringement on human rights.

No *Absolute* Freedom

Returning back to our definition of freedom: the ability to act, think, and speak however one chooses, and the state of not being imprisoned. It is easy to see how Aristotle and Rousseau provide a much more balanced approach to freedom. Absolute freedom seems to be an unattainable goal, if not for any other reason than the fact that we will eventually come up against someone who wants to do something we do not. For example, when Dana wanted to confess to being in the hit and run car, the victim's daughter asked Dana not to, because she had agreed to keep silent in exchange for money, which would provide a better life for her own children. As a result, Dana's desire to tell the truth—a right desire—was frustrated. Dana, however, is able to see that this agreement is better for the woman and her family, and so she abandons her desire to tell the truth. Aristotle would not see this as an infringement of her freedom; rather, Dana is able to act rightly in this situation, given the facts presented to her.

In this way, Aristotle and Rousseau are able to show a more nuanced concept of freedom. It is the definition of freedom that determines whether or not we are really free. It seems clear that absolute freedom would lead to chaos. If Carrie had not interfered and investigated Brody, it is possible that many more people would have died, and that his family would have been affected even more adversely. If we define freedom as the absolute ability to do whatever we want, to think whatever we want and to speak whatever we want then, no, we are not free, nor should we be.

IV

Messy Morality

8
Is There Such a Thing as Religious Violence?

ROBERTO SIRVENT AND IAN DIORIO

Whenever "terror strikes" we all stay glued to our televisions, eager to find out the perpetrator's motive. Then, when a connection to a radical Islamist group is revealed, it only confirms our suspicions. "Of course this was religiously motivated!" we exclaim. "Who else would think of needlessly killing a whole bunch of civilians?"

Violence is one thing, we tell ourselves, but *religious* violence is a different beast. It's irrational, divisive, and committed with an uncompromising devotion to an absolute God. What could be scarier? *Homeland* confronts this bias head on. It refuses to tell the typical story pitting the rational peace-loving citizens of the West against the irrational religious fanatics of the Middle East.

Discussions about religion and violence usually take one of three forms. One view claims that there's something unique about religion, like belief in God, which lends itself to violent acts. In short, these people claim that religious people are more prone to commit violence than the non-religious. A second argument is that non-religious groups, like Marxists and Nazis, can be just as violent as religious groups such as Christians and Jews. A third way of thinking about religious violence involves attempts to distinguish between authentic (peaceful) religion and inauthentic (violent) religion. We see this displayed in the episode "Breaking Hearts," where Carrie accuses Abu Nazir of perverting the teachings of Mohammed by turning teenagers into terrorists. In other words, Abu Nazir is not a *true* Muslim. A *true* Muslim would never do such a thing.

But there's a big problem with all three approaches to religious violence. They all assume a clear-cut definition of *religion*. The first camp claims that there is a distinct characteristic or set of characteristics that makes something religious. The second camp assumes this, too. Defenders of the third approach are no different since they make little attempt to question the label attached to their *religion*. Instead, they make it their goal to convince others what *true* religion looks like. In most cases, the goal is either to defend religion or to condemn it (some philosophers actually find it worthwhile to do both—and for good reason). But if people are going to debate about whether religion *causes* violence, they should probably be able to tell us what religion *is*.

Homeland is very helpful in this regard because it explores what William Cavanaugh calls "the myth of religious violence." Cavanaugh doesn't make a case for whether religion causes violence. Instead, he questions the use of the term *religion* altogether. He takes the conventional wisdom that there is *religious* violence and *secular* violence, and exposes this distinction as a myth. What does he mean by myth? A myth can be understood in many ways. It can refer to a fairytale, an outright lie, or a story told to explain where we've come and why we're here. Some myths involve all three. Here, when Cavanaugh speaks of a myth, he's referring to a certain type of story. It's a story we've all bought into. It's a story that has become so much a part of our social structure that we refuse to question it. And it's a story so widely accepted that we no longer see it as mythical, but true.

The Myth

The story we've been told is this: there is something unique about religion that makes it prone to cause violence. Religion is seen as irrational, absolutist, and divisive. It is *irrational* because religion concerns itself with the supernatural and the afterlife. Religious people don't focus on the 'here and now', so we can't expect to reason with them. We've also been told that religion is *absolutist*. By this we mean that religion demands an absolute, total, and uncompromising devotion to God. It is a devotion that is almost scary. And because religion is inherently *divisive*, the religiously devout are willing to exclude, punish, and even kill people who don't think like them.

This myth might help us explain Carrie's rash suspicion in the episode "In Memoriam." As Carrie and the gang close in on Abu Nazir, the SWAT team searches the mill but finds no trace of him. Confident that Nazir could not have escaped without some inside help, Carrie grows suspicious. Suddenly, she notices that her loyal colleague Galvez has left the scene. "Does Galvez make sense?" Quinn asks. "It might," Carrie says in one of her weakest moments. "He *is* a Muslim."

Let's take a moment to examine Carrie's train of thought here. Sure, she may have suspected Galvez because he was one of only two officers (the other being Quinn) directing the raid. Why not question Quinn? Not sure. But if she's like many people in the West, the fact that Galvez is Muslim heightens her suspicion exponentially. After all, who would be crazy enough to aid a known terrorist in attacking our country? Who would act so *irrationally*? Who would act so *violently*? All things being equal, probably a Muslim. As it turns out, Galvez was not helping Nazir. He was rushing to the hospital because his stitches ripped. Fortunately, *Homeland* chooses not to reward Carrie or its viewers for buying into the myth of religious violence.

Religion: I Know It When I See It?

So is there such a thing as religious violence? The common answer to this question is "Of course! People kill in the name of God all the time!" After all, aren't Brody and Abu Nazir committing all these terrorist acts in the name of Allah? Well, maybe. But the problem is that people mean different things when they talk about 'religion'. Scholars who study this word for a living define it in very different ways. Defining religion is not a matter of "I know it when I see it" or simply a matter of smoothing out a definition that is fuzzy around the edges. It's much more complicated than that.

There are three ways that scholars define religion. The *substantivist* approach is the most common. Substantivists, as the name suggests, tend to define religion according to the substance of your beliefs. It's the definition used whenever someone equates religion with belief in a god or gods. The *functionalist* approach to religion focuses less on what you believe and more on the way a system or ideology functions in your life. If it walks like a religion, talks like a religion, and acts like a religion, then it's a religion. Here, devotion is not measured by your beliefs but by your attitudes and actions. A conversation between Carrie and Saul in the episode "Crossfire" illustrates this well. Admiring her colleague's commitment to his job, Carrie exclaims to Saul, "You live for this shit!" Saul, aware that his absolute devotion to the CIA has resulted in his wife leaving him, replies, "So I've been told."

Both of these definitions, however, are problematic. The first (substantivism) is too narrow, since it *excludes* things like Buddhism that we want to *include* under the religion umbrella. The second (functionalism) is too broad because it *includes* things that we want to *exclude* from the category of religion. There are just too many things that function as people's religion—things like power, money, soap operas, and fantasy football. So, if we limit the term to believing in God we wipe Buddhism out of every religious textbook in the world. And if we include football, there will be no book big enough to contain such religious history.

The third approach to defining religion is called the *constructivist* approach. This approach understands the religious-secular distinction as an invention, or *construction*, of the modern West. "Religion is not simply found, but invented," Cavanaugh writes. "The term has been used in different times and places by different people according to different interests." The word religion comes from the term *religio*. But for people like Augustine (354–430), *religio* meant an attitude of respect or devotion towards a whole host of things: your neighbor, God, community, or even hobbies. The word was also used to describe different sorts of monastic rule. It meant nothing close to how we use the term today. A constructivist understands religion as having nothing unique or distinct from so-called secular ideologies and institutions. Religion is not something 'out there' that we can spot in every culture and every point in history. Rather, religion is whatever the people in power say it is. The label is assigned to groups by a particular culture, at a particular point in history, for the purpose of exercising its power in a particular way.

The Rational Us and the Irrational Them

John Locke (1632–1704), one of the main thinkers during the Enlightenment, or the "Age of Reason," played a pivotal role in shaping the myth of religious violence. For Locke, religion is a state of mind and therefore cannot be controlled by the government. To ensure peace, Locke argued for a division between the private affairs of the church and the public affairs of the state. The church could retain the citizen's *private* loyalty, but her public loyalty lay with the state. In other words, Brody and Galvez can pray to Allah all they want, but they better do so in their basement. And they better not mix their religion with more secular (and rational) matters like politics. The Enlightenment, then, put the state in charge of taming religion, especially the ones that won't stay in their proper private place. The "peaceful" religions were those that set themselves snugly under the wing of state power.

How does this way of looking at the religious and secular spheres benefit people in power? One way is that it makes it easier to justify violence committed by the nation-state. If the secular is defined as *rational* and the religious is defined as *irrational*, then we consider acts committed by secular groups as rational and acts considered by religious groups as irrational. In some cases (like torture or terrorism), it doesn't even matter if it's the *exact same act*. The religion-secular distinction profoundly shapes the way we view violence—one type of violence is seen as rational and the other is not. Religious violence is crazy and fanatical; secular violence makes sense. Religious violence focuses on salvation and eternity; secular violence focuses on the here and now. Religious violence wages war; secular violence brings peace. Ultimately, the made-up distinction of religious and secular blinds the nation-state to its own irrationality, absolutism, and divisiveness. *Homeland* certainly testifies to this.

Blind Spots

The myth of religious violence blinds us to our own fanaticism and violence. *Homeland* is at its best when it exposes these blind spots, especially as they involve double standards in American foreign policy. No scene illustrates the myth of religious violence more clearly than the Iran-Israel debate between Dana and her classmates in the episode "The Smile." Having patiently waited his turn, one student rises up to speak. "The Arab religion doesn't value human life the way we do," he says. Interrupting her classmate, Dana reminds him that Iranians are *Persians*, not *Arabs*. To this, her classmate replies, "Persians, Arabs—what's the difference? They both want the same thing, which is to annihilate us. Why shouldn't we hit them first? Maybe with a nuke or two of our own." Dana then points out the blind spot. "And what about mass murder? Do we tolerate that? I mean, because that's what he's really saying, isn't it? He's talking about turning Tehran into a parking lot." In other words, it's crazy when a religious group wants to blow up millions of people, but completely reasonable when a nation-state wants to.

This scene exposes us to a harsh reality: there is no reason to think that belief in Jesus Christ or Allah is more prone to be irrational, divisive, or absolutist than secular ideologies like nationalism. It is both interesting and disturbing that Dana's classmate shares the same foreign policy vision as well-known atheist Sam Harris. In his 2004 book, *The End of Faith*, Harris writes:

> There is little possibility of our having a *cold* war with an Islamist regime armed with long-range nuclear weapons. . . . In such a situation, the only thing likely to ensure our survival may be a nuclear first strike of our own. Needless to say, this would be an unthinkable crime—as it would kill tens of millions of innocent civilians in a single day—but it may be the only course of action available to us, given what Islamists believe.

This is what happens when we come to see other groups as irrational and violent and ourselves as reasonable and peaceful. It is also what happens when we become *absolutely* devoted to our cause, whether it's freedom, democracy, the constitution, or a desire to feel protected from people we don't understand. We become blind to our own irrationality and divisiveness. William Cavanaugh, in an obviously sarcastic tone, calls Harris's logic "impeccable" in his 2009 book, *The Myth of Religious Violence*:

> If religious people hold irrational beliefs so fervently that they will do violence for them, then there's no use trying to reason with them. They can only be dealt with by force. The myth of religious violence thus becomes justification for the use of violence. We will have peace once we have bombed the Muslims into being reasonable.

The difference between religious violence and secular violence is even harder to see in the episode "Broken Hearts" where Abu Nazir holds Carrie captive. After Carrie realizes that her attempt to reason with him falls short, Nazir says, "Do you have the perseverance, the tenacity, the faith? Because we do. It may take a century, two centuries, three centuries, but we will exterminate you." Carrie wastes no time and calls him a terrorist. This never-ending aspect of Abu Nazir's plan, we think, only confirms the existence of a religious war. It's being fought for 'higher' ends and ends that continue beyond the grave. America's war, however, is being fought for mundane ends and focuses only on the here and now.

But is it really? In the episode "In Memoriam," Carrie condemns Nazir because "his only answer is perpetual war."

Where's the blind spot, you ask? Consider the United States' war on terror. How is this *not* a perpetual war? There is no end in sight. Or consider the first name given by the United States' military for the war in Afghanistan: Mission Infinite Justice (later changed to Operation Enduring Freedom). A mission to bring *infinite* justice is hardly mundane. And it's hardly only about the here and now.

Blind spots are everywhere in *Homeland*. When Abu Nazir recruits soldiers to die for an ultimate cause, it's called brainwashing. When the American president does, it's called national defense. We find another example in the episode appropriately titled "Blind Spot." There, Brody asks Carrie if the CIA plans to torture the detainee who had previously tortured him. "We don't do that here," Carrie replies. Immediately after this exchange, we see a flashback of the detainee torturing Brody. "This is for my friends in Guantanamo," the man says, referring to the prison where U.S. officials used torture as an interrogation technique.

In the episode "Broken Hearts," Abu Nazir points out yet another American double standard, this one dealing with terrorism. "Imagine you are sitting down to dinner, with your wife and children," Nazir tells Carrie. "Out of the sky, as if thrown by an angry god, a drone strike hits, and destroys all of them. Who is the terrorist?"

What's *Really* Going On?

People kill for lots of reasons, and the myth of religious violence makes it easier to overlook this fact. The myth serves as an interpretive shortcut. It prevents us from finding out what's *really* going on. This is not to excuse the behavior of Christians and Muslims and it is not to trivialize the role their holy texts or doctrines might play in contributing to violence. It only means that we recognize other factors as well, especially those that are historical and observable. For example, it's comforting for Carrie, Saul, and the rest of the CIA to pin the source of Abu Nazir's militaristic impulses on some crazy belief in a violent God. It's not so comforting to pin it on America's violent drone strike that killed 89 innocent children. When Estes and his CIA team gather names of new terrorists and terrorist cells, it's pretty convenient to blame this on the prayer habits of radical Muslims. It's less convenient to blame it on America's habit of torturing prisoners in Guantanamo.

To clarify this point, it's worth re-visiting Dana's class debate. There, we're faced with a kid who doesn't know the difference between Persians and Arabs. And why does he need to? If you buy into the myth of religious violence, the only thing you need to know is that those people *out there* believe in something *out there* that makes them incredibly violent. If they're crazy religious fanatics, then they're going to act in crazy violent ways. It doesn't matter how our foreign policy has harmed their way of life. It doesn't matter if *they* view *us* as terrorists for blowing up a bunch of kids. And it doesn't matter if they're Persian or Arab. All that matters is that they're religious.

Constructing the categories of religious and secular meant constructing a new *us* and *them*. To reject the religious-secular distinction is to reject the violence that this distinction creates and overlooks. It also forces us to see the good in the other and the evil in ourselves. In the episode "Crossfire" we find wise words from an unexpected source—Abu Nazir. "We only begin as enemies because that's what others told us to be."

9
Afraid to Get Your Hands Dirty?

CHRISTOPHE POROT AND CHARLES TALIAFERRO

Hypocrisy is an homage that vice pays to virtue.

—FRANÇOIS DE LA ROCHEFOUCAULD

There is a darkness and mystery at the heart of *Homeland*: everyone in the show seems to lie and deceive at least one other person. According to Ken Collins, one of the directors of *Homeland*, "the ethics of hypocrisy and deceit is one of the show's central themes."

Political theorist Ruth Grant defines hypocrisy as "the pretext of virtue, idealism, or sympathetic concern used to further selfish ends." A hypocrite isn't somebody who is merely weak-willed. Imagine two people commit adultery. Both claim that they think adultery is wrong, but one person doesn't really think adultery is wrong. Imagine one merely pretends to support monogamy or condemns betrayal and deceit, but the other actually believes adultery is wrong and feels guilt and shame for the action. The first is a hypocrite whereas the second is, instead, unwilling or unable to live up to their ideals. And even though hypocrisy is deceitful, the concepts of hypocrisy and of deceit remain distinct.

Someone may deceive without lying. Similar to the hypocrisy case, a doctor may deceive a patient when she tells the patient that they have only six months to live from a seemingly incurable disease. If a cure is found that week and the patient lives a long and healthy life then the doctor technically deceived her patient. However, no one would say she was being deceptive or lying to her patient because she did not misrepresent the information she had available to her.

Walden's Selfish Ends

Homeland shows instances of both hypocrisy and deceit generally. Vice President Walden acted hypocritically when he denied any responsibility for a drone strike he ordered, a strike that killed Abu Nazir's son and many other innocent children. In response, Brody, morally outraged by Walden's hypocrisy, deceived the public and the political elite when he embraced the persona of an American Hero. Yet he embraced that image in order to execute a terrorist attack that reflects his commitment to a cause, an evidently unjust cause, but a cause not necessarily related to his "selfish ends."

Neither of these examples justifies deceit. In the first case Walden is deceitful for selfish ends and in the second Brody is deceitful to secure the success of a terrorist attack. Nonetheless, deceit, whether hypocritical or otherwise, may remain a necessary feature of politics: Edmund Burke, Machiavelli, and Rousseau are counted among the philosophers who believe deceit is a necessary compromise to make in the messy world of politics.

There are two related levels of ethical evaluation for hypocrisy and deceit. The first is societal: can a whole society benefit from some deception or hypocrisy? The second is the character of the individual wielding a sword of deceit: can an individual preserve her integrity and virtues while being deceitful, even hypocritical? At first glance it may seem unlikely, yet individuals often act hypocritically without feeling as though their integrity is compromised. When parents tell their children that Abraham Lincoln never lied, they are, themselves, lying. Ironically, they are lying to teach their kids to tell the truth. Is this simply a self-defeating act or a justifiable inconsistency? We believe it is a justifiable inconsistency, when appropriately understood.

Co-operation without Coercion

You may think that the case for deceit rests on the need to fool your enemies. It appears easy to justify deceit through the ethical codes that comprise modern Just War Theory. For instance: to defend the lives of innocent children is it not okay to lie about where they are hiding? In reality, however, some of the most interesting defenses of deception apply to relationships that stand somewhere between enemies and friends: allies.

Niccolò Machiavelli (1469–1527) makes his case for hypocrisy in a section of his famous work *The Prince* that is devoted to the prince's relations with subjects and friends. Political relationships, unlike either true friendships or open enemies, require hypocrisy because they are relationships of dependence among people with conflicting interests. Even a very powerful prince, for example, will find himself at various times in need of allies and supporters. His dependence on them makes it necessary for him to flatter them and to appear trustworthy. He needs their voluntary co-operation because he's not in a position to coerce their compliance. Yet he cannot simply expect that their co-operation will be forthcoming, because their interests do not coincide with his own.

Homeland is thick with Machiavellian scenarios. Selfish desires dictate the behavior of several key characters. Even those motivated by unselfish ends find their goals in conflict with the others who surround them. This kind of working environment rules out the possibility of an idealistic portrait of politics.

Saul acknowledges deception between allies in a political context and the distinction between allies and friends. He chides Carrie for establishing surveillance on Nick Brody without his permission. With a powerful delivery and a disappointed tone of voice, he contends in the episode "Clean Skin":

> Everyone lies in this business, I accept that. But we all draw lines somewhere, and the two sides of that line are Us and Them. And

whatever we had, you and I, whatever trust we built up over a decade of me protecting you and teaching you everything I know, you destroyed it when you lied to me and you treated me like them. Like every other schmuck in this building. So when you say you understand, is that what you mean?

If you read carefully, it's clear that Saul's understanding of the time to lie and the time to be honest is very similar to Machiavelli's. With true friends, you can be honest. And Saul thought Carrie was a true friend.

Honest Politics

There's an alternative to the politics of hypocrisy and *Homeland* actually assumes the context for it. The concept of honest politicking is rooted in the belief that one could transfer the model of economic rationality from the market to the political realm. Imagine if David Estes never tried to persuade anybody that Brody should be assassinated on moral grounds. What if he opened himself up to a trade scenario where he explains the threat posed to his selfish ends and seeks someone willing to trade that assassination for a political favor? Estes could drop the pretext of morality altogether. Would this not resolve a few problems and be a moral upgrade from his hypocritical behavior?

Also, what if Walden never covered up for his son's manslaughter? What if Walden openly acknowledged the violation of justice and the public was capable and willing to tolerate it because it would not change their minds about voting for him? Instead of voters holding the man culpable by moral standards, they would simply evaluate whether or not he could successfully satisfy their interests if he was in office. If he could, then he would remain in office, and justice for his son's victim would not have been obstructed.

According to this way of looking at it, hypocrisy and deceit are products of an unwillingness to be honest about our basic human nature and needs. We have to pretend to be moral, but that false pretext actually makes us less moral rather than more moral.

The honest politicking model, rooted in eighteenth-century economic theory, shares an understanding of human nature with the famous economic philosopher Adam Smith (1723–1790). According to Smith, humans have a natural propensity to barter and trade with each other and his theory is popularized as an endorsement of human selfishness and the benefits it could breed if we allow it to move the market: "It is not from the benevolence of the butcher, the brewer, or the baker that we expect our dinner but from their regard to their own interest. We address ourselves, not to their humanity but to their self-love, and never talk to them of our own necessities but of their advantages." In this framework, honest exchanges are not only more aligned with human nature, but they also create the conditions for a more effective political universe.

Not Gonna Work

However, there are many reasons why we believe economic rationality can't work in politicking.

First, the economic model fails because it already assumes the moral bankruptcy of the project at hand. In a world where no one actually cares about securing moral ends, it makes more sense to rely on human rationality and self-interest than on virtues. Virtues would become an unnecessary roadblock to the ultimate goal of securing an individual's private interest.

Nonetheless, politics is about securing the public good. So even if there are selfish individuals within the system or instances where selfish desire triumphs over public good, it ought to be the goal of politics to secure that public good.

When Carrie assumes the moral bankruptcy of the person she is co-operating with, she willingly resorts to an honest politick. For instance, in "Representative Body" when she was dealing with the corrupt Saudi diplomat, Al Sahrani, who was accepting money for aiding terrorism, she resorted to threatening his interests instead of explaining the moral significance of the situation to him. Rather than arguing that he would be saving lives by co-operating with the CIA, she threatens to reveal sensitive information that would destroy his career if he refused to co-operate. While this is a case of blackmail, and thus widely considered an immoral use of basic incentives, it's still an example of Carrie appealing to private interests rather than the public good when the situation demands it.

In such a situation, the actor being incentivized was already assumed to have no interest in morality, and therefore the project of securing the public good, for the sake of the public good, was already dropped. Instead of dropping the project altogether, we believe it's better to balance selfish-interest with the public good. Thus, even if someone is attempting to secure their own selfish interest they are required to adjust their position to the contours of a morally acceptable action.

Paying Homage

The great French thinker François de la Rochefoucauld (1613–1680) believed in a similar principle when he quipped: "Hypocrisy is an homage that vice pays to virtue." He means that hypocrisy may require truly selfish individuals to behave in ways that benefit the public good, even if they are only doing so to promote their personal reputation and power. Imagine a CEO of a corporation that is solely dedicated to maximizing profit. In order to garner publicity and capture public support for his organization, he donates money to a children's hospital. He would not have donated that money if the public felt morality was just a barrier to exchanges of rational self-interest. In this way, he was forced to do something good even if it did not make him a good person.

In "Game On" Saul capitalizes on this scenario and beautifully expresses the tension between the public good and private interest when he strong-armed a judge to give him legal authority for surveillance on a terrorist suspect. Saul only wanted the surveillance because he was concerned about the safety of citizens. However, the judge was concerned about his personal reputation, so what did Saul do? He threatened the judge's reputation in order to motivate him to do the, ostensibly, right thing. In response to the discomfort of the situation, the judge says, "Can we at least pretend this is about The Law?" to which Saul brilliantly responds, "This is about The Law."

The point made is that the ultimate purpose of the exchange was not to preserve the Judge's reputation but, instead, to do the right thing. Hypocrisy was instrumentalized for the public good rather than making the public good subservient to hypocrisy. It's difficult to untangle the web of ethical problems arising from the examples we chose to use, but it remains the case that *Homeland*'s most virtuous characters, Carrie and Saul, appear to be on board with the necessity of deceit and hypocrisy. And, it appears, the urgency of the terrorist attacks they face and the unethical context they are surrounded by forces them, though themselves virtuous, to compromise a pure ethic of honesty.

Good? Right?

Even if the political context of *Homeland* appears to demand the use of deceit and hypocrisy, there remains a more fundamental ethical question: does something's necessity make it also morally "good" or "right?" The answer to this question divides philosophers.

At one end of the spectrum are pure consequentialists who believe that the appropriate ends can justify any means. If one must drop a nuclear weapon to save the rest of the world then it would be moral to drop the weapon and immoral not to. We believe there is something unsatisfying about this answer: anything and everything can be considered moral based on the outcome. If we must kill in order to save lives, does that mean that the individual we kill had a life without value? Is it really morally okay to kill, even if the end good is greater than the harm caused?

On the other end of the spectrum are pure deontological thinkers who believe that one must do what is right simply because it is the right thing to do and, therefore, no ends can justify the means. The German philosopher Immanuel Kant (1724–1804) controversially contended that moral laws are unconditional. So, according to Kant, in the case of a Nazi soldier asking where you are hiding Jewish children, you ought to tell the truth.

Part of Kant's concern stems from the fact that consequentialist behavior assumes that you know how things will turn out, which he believes we can't know. We can only know the moral laws themselves. So, perhaps the children have already escaped and honesty would help them rather than harm them, or perhaps the Nazi soldiers are actually Allies in disguise and it's their intention to save the children. By lying to whom you think are Nazis you have both worsened the situation and violated a moral law.

Carrie encountered this problem in "Clean Skin" when she lied to Lynne Reed, a CIA informant who might have been able to acquire more information about Abu Nazir's next plot. Reed asked for reassurance for her safety in order to proceed with her missions, but Carrie lied by telling her she was being protected when she wasn't, because Carrie believed that Reed would ultimately acquire useful information and everyone would be safe. Unfortunately, Reed was killed and unable to acquire information. She was only in harm's way because of Carrie's lie, which was based on a false understanding of the situation.

While this is a serious concern, we do have to act on limited knowledge. If we offer food to a starving man it's possible that the food may have been poisoned or that he may choke on the dinner. Yet, that should not stop us from offering the food—we take those risks based on the best information we have. And if the situation seems sufficiently clear, we believe it would be a good thing to consider the consequences of one's actions as well as the morality of the action's themselves.

Dirty Hands

There is an approach to ethical decisions that helps us to re-solve the tension between doing what has good outcomes and doing what is morally good in itself. It's known as the 'Dirty Hands' tradition, and it dates back to Machiavelli, though its present currency is largely owed to the American political theorist Michael Walzer who gave it the title of 'Dirty Hands' in an influential article from 1973 titled "Political Action: The Problem of Dirty Hands."

The Dirty Hands position shares both the assumption that certain actions are wrong in themselves and the conclu-sion that they are nonetheless necessary. An action can be both morally wrong and morally right. The Christian realist Reinhold Niebuhr promotes such a position when he advo-cates for the necessity of accepting guilt even when we feel our action was justified. Thus, even if it is necessary to kill in order to save lives this does not make killing moral. The actor who killed to save lives has both done something wor-thy of moral condemnation and, through the same action, something moral.

Dirty Hands ethics are often formulated as paradoxical and self-defeating. Logically, however, the concept of Dirty Hands isn't a paradox. The same item may hold two mutu-ally conflicting properties at the same time. Imagine a circle. One side of the circle is red and the other side of the circle is blue. The circle is both red and blue, one side is red and the other is blue even though the circle cannot be entirely red and entirely blue at the same time.

Likewise, with Dirty Hands ethics, the same action may be both wrong and right. The act itself is morally wrong, but the consequences of the action are good, morally speaking. Therefore, instead of considering dirty hands a self-defeating proposition, we believe it is better understood as a layered ac-count of the phenomenon. This kind of layered account often applies to moral actions. We can reverse the scenario and imagine that someone performs a morally justifiable action with immoral consequences. Recall the example of feeding a starving homeless person only to realize that the food is poisoned. The action itself was moral but the outcome was immoral. Therefore it is easy to separate the morality of an action from the morality of the action's outcome.

We All Have Them

What makes Dirty Hands ethics difficult is that the actor must willingly perform an act that they know to be, at least partially, wrong. This is quite a burden to place on any individual. That's why it requires a certain kind of virtue: the willingness to accept the moral complexity and the related guilt of doing the right thing. In "Broken Hearts" Dar Adal asks Saul whether or not he is "still afraid to get his hands dirty." That moment captures the essence of the show: many people are compromising the worthy ethic of honesty in order to pursue the moral end of protecting innocent civilian lives. It's important that we don't conflate what is necessary with what is morally sound and we believe the characters in *Homeland* all have some "dirty hands."

V

Dealing with Drones

10
Drones and Terrorist Blowback

JAI GALLIOTT

I have a confession to make. Like millions of other viewers, I tune in every week to get my dose of *Homeland,* delivered through Showtime's pop culture syringe. The show's writers have worked in a narrative that seamlessly fuses with what we imagine to be "real life."

In any given week, you'd be forgiven for mistaking something you watched on *Homeland* with some atrocity that you read about in the *New York Times* or spotted on your Twitter feed. The show's also a hit with the DC crowd, including President Obama himself, who has also confessed to having an addiction and retreating to the Oval Office to fuel it each Saturday when Michelle and his girls go out to play tennis. Others have taken it to the woodshed for what is often called a lack of "verisimilitude," which is a nice way of saying that some critics think it makes no fuckin' sense. These critics seem to ignore the fact that beyond the plot and character mayhem, *Homeland* sends a number of very consistent messages in taking a fictionalized dive into matters like the CIA's secrecy and PTSD's impact on war veterans. Its writers also seem to have some very strong views about the use of "unmanned aerial vehicles," also known as "drones."

Drones from Day One

The show depicts a former US marine by the name of Sgt. Brody, a POW turned terrorist turned sympathetic antihero. Although terrorist leader Abu Nazir held Brody captive and had him tortured for eight years in Afghanistan, Brody eventually becomes Nazir's devotee. He also comes to care for his Afghan captor's young son, Issa, whom he has been teaching English and thinking of as his own.

Brody is severely traumatized when a drone strike, ordered secretly by the Vice President, kills Issa and eighty-two other young students in his madrassa. He is "turned" by this act, which fuels his vengeful motives for plotting against the United States. Eventually, at Nazir's behest, Brody returns to the US with orders to wipe out the Vice President and other key heads of government by way of a suicide bomb. The point here is that drones are at the core of all that has gone wrong in *Homeland*. Drones killed Issa. Drones killed all the other innocent children. Drones turned Brody.

At the same time, the show makes for some great propaganda by constructing the CIA and its spies as the good guys in all the unfolding melodrama. The agency itself is portrayed as being constantly on the defensive in our Era of Terror. The show's writers would have us think that it's populated with people of good will and benevolent intent, who focus on counter-terrorism operations at great personal cost. We need only witness Carrie's constant struggle with bipolar disorder or the complicated love affairs that stem from Saul's willingness to go above and beyond the call of duty for the agency.

The real CIA, of course, has a long and fairly dark history of off-the-books black ops, dodgy weapons sales, global narcotics operations, drone warfare and other controversial actions that were deemed necessary by the higher echelons but kept hidden from public view until the consequences of these projects could no longer be hidden. While credit must be given to *Homeland* for tackling the matter, it is not as though the drone strike we saw in the first season was a one-off incident with some unusual "blowback" consequences, as the writers have attempted to pass it off. In reality, this kind of thing is an almost daily occurrence that needs to be considered within the context of a decade-long and largely secret US war that killed thousands of innocent people in the greater Middle East.

But dude, it's just a television show. Take it easy. Right? Wrong. We need to ensure that with so many people addicted to the drama of *Homeland* and America addicted to what it shortsightedly sees as soldier-saving drones, we don't risk underestimating the potential downsides and ignoring the innocent lives, tax dollars and collective future at stake. While the US now has a left-center or liberal president at the helm, it's sending more drones into conflict than ever before. Recent figures suggest that Obama orders a drone strike one in every four days as opposed to Bush, who only ordered one in every ten. As viewers tune in for their weekly hit, it's important that they watch it critically and consider if the good guys–bad guys line is in the right place and whether the "good guys" are pursuing the desired ends through the right means.

The Drone Problem Explained

Some big and powerful state has what it thinks is a good reason for going to war (a just cause) against some small state, which has a right to try and defend itself as they dispute the claims underlying their opponent's just cause. The "big guy" uses many drones of the kind that killed Issa, but the "little guy" lacks a drone arsenal and cannot respond in kind. What's more, because the war is unmanned, the little guy can't retaliate in the "normal way" by targeting troops engaged on the ground in the "business of war." In exercising its right to self-defense, the little guy wants to act in an ethically sanctioned manner as it derives its power from its people and they have a vested interest in acting morally, but it is limited in its pursuit of ethical aims and must therefore seek alternative ways of dealing with and responding to the unmanned attack. It is these alternatives we must work through to form some idea of what the response and its probable effects are likely to be and whether an attack like this remains, in light of this forward-looking projection, the most effective and most ethical option for the real world equivalent of Vice President Walden.

The main problem is that where there's a radical imbalance in power created by one side holding all the cool military gadgets, there's only a limited number of options open to the weaker state once we have ruled out the extraordinarily unlikely option of them laying down arms. In the example above, the big guy can quite easily locate and attack the little guy's combatants because they are likely to be wearing uniforms and bearing arms that will stand out like a Naval officer in an Army mess. The same task is made rather difficult for the little guy because of their enemy's purely technological presence. This gives rise to an ethically concerning potentiality called the 'guerrilla problem' that's played out in just about every episode of *Homeland*. In order to avoid being targeted and possibly killed by their opponents with all the high-tech weapons, they will try to conceal themselves and their weapons amongst the vulnerable civilian population. This tactic has the effect of making it much more difficult and potentially dangerous for drone-wielding Westerners to abide by the just war principles of discrimination and proportionality, which most robe-wearing philosophers take to mean that we must not target innocent people and only engage in military action proportionate to the harm done. For weak states, the aim is often to provoke the enemy and then comingle with the civilian population in the hope that they will be driven to continue with attacks that cause a large number of civilian casualties and other collateral damage, something Saul-types valiantly try to limit.

Drones on Your Doorstep

However, the little guys are not alone in utilizing asymmetric tactics like this and shifting the burden of risk onto their civilian populations. Drone pilots are regularly comingled with civilians.

The most well-known US drone command center operates from the CIA's not-so-secret headquarters in Langley, Virginia, whilst Nevada's Creech and Nellis Air Force bases near Las Vegas house more military operations. Domestic bases also operate in California, Arizona, New Mexico, North and South Dakota, Missouri, Ohio, New York, and perhaps elsewhere. In early 2013, Fox News even reported that new jobs and drone technology are coming to the former Willow Grove Naval Air Station in Horsham, Pennsylvania. While it was never planned for aircraft to fly out of the base, the plans prompted community groups to launch their own campaign against the multi-million-dollar command center and the extension of the battlefield into their own backyards.

But are drone pilots combatants and thus appropriate targets for their enemies? This is an important question because while a good deal has been said about PTSD and protecting those abroad who may be vulnerable to drone strikes, little has been said about protecting those civilians amongst the operators of drones. A drone operator who actively tracks and kills enemies is targetable as a participant in combat. However, for a large number of drone operators, their civilian and military worlds are intertwined. Moral problems arise when an operator finishes their shift and goes home.

We need to think carefully about whether drone operators are targetable when they are eating, sleeping, and picking up the children from school. While normal combatants do not acquire immunity when they eat or sleep and cannot simply "turn off" their combatant status, as drones proliferate around the world and wars become an increasingly part-time endeavor for those engaged to fight them, we may be forced to reconsider what it means to be a combatant.

Whether or not we consider State X's drone pilots to be combatants, any story of the technological asymmetry that accompanies the widespread deployment of unmanned systems and the shielding of military assets will necessarily include those in the civilian realm being exposed to what some might perceive to be an unfair level of risk. This is a recurring theme in Andrew Croome's *Midnight Empire*, an espionage thriller that deftly explores drone warfare. In this novel of modern warfare, an Australian drone programmer relocates to the United States to work with a drone team operating at Creech Air Force base. Soon after he arrives, however, American drone pilots start to die in the usually peaceful residential suburbs of Las Vegas, as their targets become the targeters.

Far from delivering safer and more effective remote warfare, drones actually bring the battle home and put those who wage it more closely among us than ever before. Over the long term, this may well bring the citizens of warring states together out of sympathy for each other, but is only likely to inspire hatred in the nearer term. In this case, the killing of drone pilots may not be considered a violation of present-day just war theory, but radical technological disparities may also evoke further anger and actions that closely resemble classical domestic terrorism and play out in real life rather than in books or on the screen.

The evidence suggests that drone strikes only strengthen the terrorist cause, making the al Qaeda brand and radical Islam more attractive to vulnerable and disaffected American Muslims like Brody. He's not alone either. Think about the two young Boston Marathon bombers, who cited the drone wars in Iraq and Afghanistan as a motivating factor for their attack. Cases like this only confirm the idea that drones create more terrorists than the number of enemy combatants that they kill.

Soldiers, statesmen, and television viewers must, therefore, add a corollary to their theorem: if one side uses a large fleet of drones against which the enemy has no real defense, the victims may reciprocate by utilizing tactics that render the technologically superior state comparably defenseless. It is not immediately clear whether these tactics will, in all cases, be contrary to the demands of just war theory or unfair on civilians. On the first point there is much debate concerning whether terrorist action can meet just war requirements.

On the latter, it needs to be admitted that citizens of the West are the ultimate source of casualty adverseness and responsible for electing the Waldens of the world who authorize war on our behalf, thus they may be forced to accept that that potential terrorist "blowback" is simply a concerning but necessary feature of the only sort of warfare they are prepared to sanction. That said, in drone wars, violations of the laws of war are much more likely to occur on either side of the conflict. This may tip the proportionality scale against the waging of war in the first instance. That is, if these al-Qaeda and Brody-style responses can be foreseen, it may again undermine the moral justification for a state's actions. If there is cause to suggest that provoking the little guy might result in its appealing to these morally questionable options, then the big guys must think more carefully about what it stands to gain from going to war.

Demanding, Yeah?

Some might object to the level of foresight I'm demanding from our head honchos. Let me summarize before you criticize: the little guy is doing this bad thing (prosecuting a war with what its opponent sees as unjust aims) and then, because its stronger opponent uses drones as their means of waging war, this leads to the little guy doing this further bad thing (in this case, harming people near where the drones operated from). It might be said that this is neither an argument against the strong state or, for that matter, the use of drones. Some folks have told me that it would require a very high degree of certainty that using drones, which has other normative advantages, would necessarily lead to this sort of terrorist blowback. Some have argued that even if this can be assured, the moral blame here still falls on the little guy doing this bad thing, not on the big guy for pursuing some just action via putatively just means.

In response to the first portion of this argument, the degree of certainty involved is already high, with *Homeland* and a number of recent homeland terrorist attacks serving as a potent reminder of the fact that technological asymmetry does not preclude enemies with inferior technology from creating and sustaining an effect powerful enough to combat a superpower and, in fact, asymmetry probably invites this when there are no other options for potential foes.

This is not to reassign blame, absolve anyone of moral responsibility, or open the door for any state to do bad things in the hope that they might get their enemy to cease efforts against them; instead, it is to acknowledge that the harm generated by such war comes about for predictable and identifiable reasons, as we saw with Brody. One possible response might be to suggest that the state with big boys' toys allow the weaker state a degree of latitude in their application of just war principles. However, allowing an enemy to perform less than ethically is obviously problematic and would likely lead to additional problems and serious moral transgressions. Therefore, giving the weaker state a "wild card" is not the answer.

Another much more respectable and less problematic approach is for the stronger state to impose stronger requirements on its own applications or consideration of the just war principles already mentioned. This involves the stronger state in having to meet higher standards of certainty when waging war. This seems a sensible ethical option. It does not encourage the stronger state to lower protective measures, to "go easy" on the enemy or to lay down its arms, which is good because there is no virtue in taking risk purely for the sake of risk.

The Right Balance

What, then, might a war that abides by these stronger norms look like? It might look more like international policing.

In policing action, actions are based on the collection of evidence that proves guilt beyond reasonable doubt. De-escalation strategies are preferred, very little collateral damage is tolerable and the death of innocents is strictly prohibited. The effect would be to give civilians much higher standing relative to drone operators, with the implication of limiting the number of strikes. However, while less war and more international policing-like activity may sound an admirable goal, some would argue this is too restrictive as a response to asymmetry and that we must continue to find the right balance.

In any case, Obama needn't do anything about his *Homeland* addiction, but he does need to think more carefully about his addiction to drones and how they affect his homeland.

11
Killing at a Distance

Edwin Jacob

Sergeant Nicholas Brody is a patriot who loves his country. Or so he says in a self-recorded confession prior to strapping on a suicide vest to take out key members of the US security circle who conducted and covered up a drone strike that missed its target and yielded substantial civilian deaths ("Marine One").

Drones have become the quintessential weapon in America's "war on terror." The drone program, run by the CIA, is based on performing "targeted killings" against terrorist figures around the world. Proponents of the program argue that drones strikes are precise, effective, and do not pose any risk on the part of fighting forces that "pilot" these vehicles from remote locations. Those who oppose drone warfare, however, argue that the program is creating more terrorists than it eliminates. Civilian casualties, they argue, are producing hatred against the US that will aid terrorist groups in their recruiting efforts. *Homeland* has effectively conveyed the uses and abuses of drones.

Ethics concerns itself with making judgments about human action. Means are the actions that are taken to arrive at a desired outcome—the end. There are two main approaches to ethics: the utilitarian and deontological. The utilitarian approach judges actions by the ends they produce. An action is considered ethical if the end or outcome is good. The means used in getting to a desired end don't really matter. The deontological approach considers that actions can be judged independently of the consequences they produce; therefore, some actions would be judged bad even if the total outcome is good. So for instance, the murder of an innocent person might be considered bad even if the total outcome were the saving of many lives.

Utilitarian by Nature

Military planning is utilitarian by nature. A straight cost-benefit analysis is brought to bear. The maximum result from the lowest cost—be it economic (the least amount of capital expenditure) or human (the lowest amount of loss of life, be it military or civilian)—is the overriding aim. Historical examples of this ethical form of warfare abound. Truman's decision to "drop the bomb" on the cities of Hiroshima and Nagasaki; indiscriminate carpet bombings of Vietnam, which were managed by McNamara in Washington; and the "shock and awe" campaign of the opening days of the Iraq invasion—all these cases illustrate what the sociologist Max Weber would call the "ethics of ultimate ends," as opposed to the "ethics of responsibility."

The joint decision to attack Abu Nazir with a drone strike was based on utilitarian thinking. Vice President Walden—the point man of the operation—is told by Deputy CIA Director Estes that there is an eighty percent chance that Nazir is in their crosshairs. When told by Estes that the target is a school, Walden responds that Nazir is the one responsible for putting the children at risk, not the US. Although a ground op is preferable to avoid loss of civilian lives, there just isn't enough time. A decision must be made. In their collective estimate, "potential collateral damage falls within current matrix parameters." The killing of Nazir is such an important end that it outweighs the civilian deaths that will occur.

Numbers don't lie. But they don't tell the whole story either. The "matrix" Walden speaks of is a formula. It assigns a *quantitative* value to eliminating Nazir and is balanced against the number of civilian deaths that are "acceptable" in achieving the goal. We are not told what number of civilian deaths would have outweighed the decision to authorize the strike that ended up killing eighty-three children, while missing the intended target. At what numerical point is "collateral damage" unacceptable? To what extent, if any, are human lives quantifiable and applicable to a cost-benefit analysis?

Brody's Road: Patriot or Enemy?

An emaciated, matted-haired, bruised, and scarred prisoner of war. This is how we are introduced to US Marine Sergeant Nicholas Brody, the antagonist or protagonist (depending on which episode you're watching) of *Homeland*. Subjected to eight years of enemy capture—which included torture, isolation, and shame—there is doubt as to whether he can be reintegrated into his pre-captured life, which includes a wife and two children. As if this wasn't bad enough, his allegiance to his country is in serious doubt, as Carrie Matheson, a CIA operative, has gained field intel, in the opening scenes of the pilot episode, that an American POW has been "turned."

The turning of Brody was not the product of torture at the hands of his captors (although, to be fair, they sure as hell tried!), but rather the result of a US action. A drone strike that missed its intended target—Abu Nazir, an al-Qaeda commander and Brody's captor—and killed eighty-three children turned Brody to his captor's side ("Crossfire"). Issa, Nazir's son, with whom Brody had formed a fatherly connection, was one of the eighty-three children who were deemed acceptable collateral damage, if it meant getting Nazir, by the US forces that approved the strike. I can't imagine that choosing the name "Issa" was an accident on the part of the show's writers. It is Arabic for "Jesus." Likewise, Issa's death can be seen as a metaphor for Brody's transformation.

Prior to strapping on a suicide vest to exact justice for Issa and the eighty-two other children who were killed in the drone attack, Brody records a confession ("Marine One"). In the tape, Brody, who is clad in his Marine uniform, which is adorned with various commendation medals, proclaims that he is a patriot who loves his country. As such, his act is, from his vantage point, one of delivering justice to a corrupt cadre of unprincipled hawks, who care only about maintaining their positions by appealing to interests of "national security."

Whereas terrorism entails immediacy, drones, by their very nature, are based on distance and, no pun intended, remoteness. This supra-spatial relationship between enemies marks the latest shift in military technology. Mechanization of war is alienating the human element in an otherwise human act that is based on one group having at one another on a field of battle. Speaking of Operation Desert Storm, Bill Hicks, the late comedian, once noted that there never was a war in Iraq. "A war is when two armies are fighting. It wasn't exactly a war." He had a point.

Asymmetric Warfare

Asymmetry has marked the American way of war since the collapse of the Soviet Union. Although asymmetric warfare has been appropriated as a defining characteristic of the "war on terror," the characterization is often one-sided. It's the terrorist who is seen as fighting us disproportionately, not the other way around. It only took nineteen hijackers to alter the foreign policy of America. (So much for the arguments that terrorism doesn't work!) Yet the US was unable to successfully quell an occupied territory in Iraq with the economic and martial means it brought to bear. Asymmetry works both ways, and the US is capitalizing on it through the drone—a technological marvel that can be deployed and controlled across the globe. This eye in the sky may see all, but what its victims see is a supercilious superpower that has lost its will to fight them head on.

Technology has always factored into warfare: The side which has the means and will to employ superior weapons against the other is the victor. This was certainly the case for David who slew Goliath with a slingshot as surely as it was for the coalition forces in the Iraq War, the latter of which has yielded a documented civilian death toll well above one hundred thousand. Yeah, one death is a tragedy, a million a statistic. If drones can turn a patriot, albeit a fictional one, like Brody into an "enemy" of the state, we had better evaluate the degree to which drone warfare may be doing more harm than good.

No Exceptions

The great Enlightenment thinker Immanuel Kant (1724–1804) believed that we can become aware of a "moral law within"—we can know that some actions are right or wrong irrespective of their consequences. He founded his deontological ethics on what he called "the categorical imperative," a moral rule that knows no exceptions. Kant gave three variations of the categorical imperative in the *Groundwork of the Metaphysic of Morals* (1785):

- Firstly, **"Act only in accordance with that maxim through which you can at the same time will that it become a universal law."**

I must reflect upon the universal implications of my act before performing it. Should I lie? Should I cheat? Should I kill? So long as I am comfortable living in a world where lying, cheating, and killing is acceptable, then my decision to commit these acts (lying, cheating, or killing) is just. If I don't desire to live in a world where these acts are permissible, however, I am ethically bound to abstain from them.

- Secondly, **"Act so that you use humanity, as much in your own person as in the person of every other, always at the same time as end and never merely as means."**

I can't treat people (or myself for that matter) as a means to an end, but rather always as an end unto itself. Being disingenuous towards others is prohibited, as is treating myself as a means to an end—hence the Kantian prohibition against suicide.

- **Thirdly, "Act in accordance with maxims of a universally legislative member for a merely possible realm of ends."**

I am the King of the Moral Universe! My actions are made in accordance with the rest of humanity, who are also moral legislators in this "kingdom of ends."

Judging the Drone and Those Who Wield It

From Kant's perspective, Walden's decision to authorize the drone strike against Nazir—knowing full well that a school full of children would be caught in the crosshairs—is an unethical act. Nazir, according to Walden, put those children in danger by virtue of living next to the school. Real world war hawks often invoke this line of reasoning. Accepting civilian deaths is the ultimate means to an end, particularly Nazir's end! Would Walden (and his cohorts) be comfortable living in an America where drone strikes—with attendant civilian deaths—were an increasingly new way of life, where nation states abuse our sovereignty to eliminate theirs? I doubt it.

Defenders of the current military practices are quick to say that we can't afford to delude ourselves that we are living in a pre-9/11 world. We have to fight them "over there," or we will end up fighting them "over here." Yet although the threat posed by terrorist groups is real, our current counterterrorist policies may not be effective—they may even be counterproductive. There is a palpable backlash against the US drone policy. Faisal Shahzad blamed America's drone attacks, as well as America's occupation of Afghanistan and Iraq, as the motive in his failed bombing effort in Times Square in December 2009. The US is seen as an enemy to both terrorist groups and civilian populations that are harmed as a result of drone strikes. Although their grievances are different, their scorn is shared, and the attacks help to form an alliance between terrorists and civilian populations.

Many Americans, with varied political outlooks, are becoming increasingly uncomfortable with the drone program. Politics indeed makes strange bedfellows. Liberals deride the program over what they see as the unlawful nature of targeted killings in foreign lands. It has been argued that sovereignty is being violated. Territorial excursions into foreign countries that have not agreed to permit the US in their air space have been openly disregarded.

The killing of Anwar and Abdulrahman al-Awlaki, American citizens both, two years ago in Yemen, raised the question of whether Americans' constitutional rights of due process stopped at the water's edge. Conservatives have been apt to warn that drones will not be limited to foreign territories. They see the drone as a potential tool for unconstitutional attacks on US citizens by the government. And the "black helicopters" that New World Order conspiracy theorists have been warning against for years may in fact be coming via the drone.

Both the deontological and the utilitarian approaches cause us to question the drone program. According to the deontological approach, there is something wrong with taking innocent life, even if the outcome—the defeat of terrorists—is good. However, we can also question whether the drone attacks are on balance effective, if they encourage the victims to become future terrorists.

We have a choice to make. Will we accept military strategies that, at the very least, strain the credulity of ethical and legal norms to maintain a semblance that we are winning the "war on terror"? This policy is hitting a hornet's nest in the process of swatting flies. If 9/11 has taught us anything, it is that US military intervention can lead to "blowback," where foreigners with a grievance attack the US. Our next generation of enemies may be brewing in a cauldron of our own making.

Bleeding to Leading

Reports of the latest drone strike—be it in Afghanistan, Pakistan, or Yemen—fill the pages of news media. As the old newspaper adage says, "If it bleeds it leads." What the media rarely pursue is the extent to which this strategy is actually useful in achieving its intended results. Worse, ethical dimensions of this form of warfare have not entered the discourse in a meaningful way. Kant was surely right when he said that he who "wills the end, also wills the means that are indispensably necessary to it that are in his control." Peace is the end. The means employed to reach that end is, ultimately, what counts.

VI

Covert Speculations

12
It's Epistemic War Out There!

DON FALLIS

In his *Meditations on First Philosophy*, René Descartes famously asks whether there is anything that we can know for sure. While I certainly seem to know that I am "moving my head and stretching out my hands," I can't be sure that I'm not just dreaming. In fact, I can't even be sure that there are such things as heads and hands because there might be "some malicious demon of the utmost power and cunning that has employed all his energies in order to deceive me." Of course, nobody (including Descartes) thinks that such a demon really exists.

The television series *Homeland*, however, depicts a world in which there really are beings that employ all their energies to deceive us. Unfortunately, with global terrorism and the modern surveillance state that has grown up in response, it is the world in which all of us now live. Foreign terrorists and agents of our own government are constantly trying to make the world appear to be one way when it is really another.

Homeland provides numerous examples of this sort of *epistemic warfare* (as the contemporary philosopher Peter Ludlow calls it). Sergeant Nicholas Brody gets everyone—or almost everyone—to think that he's a war hero rather than a terrorist working for al-Qaeda. CIA agent Carrie Mathison convinces Brody that she is just another veteran attending a support group and not someone who has been following him for days ("Semper I"). She also hides from her bosses at the CIA the fact that she has Brody under surveillance as soon as he returns to the United States and the fact that she has a serious psychiatric disorder. Abu Nazir tricks Brody into believing that he beat Tom Walker to death while they were both held captive by al-Qaeda ("Achilles Heel"). Saul Berenson smuggles a memory card containing Brody's incriminating video out of Beirut by making a Lebanese security official believe that he has found the only copy in Saul's luggage ("State of Independence").

A World of Liars and Deceivers

Although the term *epistemic warfare* is fairly new, philosophers have been studying this topic for centuries. *Epistemology* is the area of philosophy that looks at how we can acquire knowledge about the world. Sometimes, we fail to achieve this goal simply because we're not careful enough in our investigations or because we're accidentally misled. But as *Homeland* makes clear, there may be someone out there who is *actively* trying to deceive us.

In addition to Descartes, several epistemologists have addressed this particular (and particularly dangerous) threat to knowledge. For instance, in *An Enquiry Concerning Human Understanding*, David Hume discusses what to do when someone tells you something surprising: "I immediately consider with myself, whether it be more probable, that this person should either deceive or be deceived, or that the fact, which he relates, should really have happened."

The Logic of Covert Operations

Epistemic warfare has gotten very sophisticated in recent years. It often involves the use of advanced information and computer technology. For instance, as Ludlow points out, private intelligence agencies have developed systems for the government "that allow one user to control multiple online identities ("sock puppets") for commenting in social media spaces, thus giving the appearance of grass roots support."

However, deception in *Homeland* tends to be less hi-tech. It typically just involves a person pretending to be another sort of person. In addition to Brody's pretenses, another terrorist (Roya Hammad) pretends to be a journalist, another terrorist (Tom Walker) pretends to be a homeless person, and yet another terrorist (Raqim Faisel) pretends to be a university professor. (Roya actually is a journalist, but she is not *merely* a journalist as she pretends to be. Similarly, Faisel is not merely a professor.) And, of course, the good guys as well as the bad guys misrepresent themselves. In addition to Carrie's pretenses, a CIA black-ops agent (Peter Quinn) pretends to be just another CIA analyst. (Quinn does work for the United States government, but not quite in the capacity that he leads Carrie and Saul to believe.)

Such covert operations (or "covert ops") go back a long way. A notable example is the large wooden horse that the Greeks left in front of the gates of ancient Troy. It appeared to be an offering to the gods, but it actually concealed Greek soldiers who only revealed themselves once the horse had been wheeled inside the city walls. In fact, Brody himself is intended by Nazir to be a Trojan Horse of sorts. The plan is for Brody to be rescued from captivity in Afghanistan and welcomed back into the United States (and ultimately into a bunker with the Vice President) where he will wreak havoc as a suicide bomber.

Make That a Double

But even old-fashioned covert operations can get quite complicated. In addition to *covert operatives* who pretend to be something that they are not, there are *double agents* who pretend to be covert operatives. When the CIA convinces him to switch sides, Brody becomes a double agent, *only pretending* to work for Nazir after that point ("Q&A"). Moreover, after Brody comes back from his unexpected helicopter trip to see Nazir, the CIA is worried that Brody might only be pretending to be a double agent ("Two Hats"). In other words, he could have become a "triple agent" or a "re-doubled agent."

As Saul points out, "By his own admission, Brody's in a confused state. Spent twelve hours in the company of a man who has considerable power over him." Thus, David Estes wisely concludes, "We need to be extremely fucking vigilant here."

To be precise though, I should really define a double agent as someone who pretends to be a covert operative *for a particular organization*. He is not someone who pretends to be a covert operative *period*. A double agent *is* a covert operative. He is just a covert operative for a different organization from the one for which he is pretending to be a covert operative. While Brody is only pretending to be a covert operative for Nazir once he has been turned, Brody is still a covert operative for the CIA.

Furthermore, this example serves to illustrate that—as philosophers often emphasize—it's important to be careful in defining our terms. If a double agent were someone who pretended to be a covert operative *period*, we would have a contradiction along the lines of Russell's Paradox. Bertrand Russell devised this paradox in order to show that Gottlob Frege's work in set theory was inconsistent. Russell famously illustrated the paradox by imagining a barber who shaves everyone in town who does not shave themselves. To see the paradox, just ask yourself who shaves the barber.

To see the "Double Agent Paradox," ask yourself whether a double agent is a covert operative. If he is a covert operative, then he is what he pretends to be. So, he is not pretending to be something that he is not. Thus, by definition, he is not a covert operative. However, if he is not a covert operative, then he *is* pretending to be something that he is not (when he pretends to be a covert operative). So, by definition, he is a covert operative. (This paradox is basically the same as the "Charlatan Paradox" that the logician Raymond Smullyan describes in *The Gödelian Puzzle Book*.)

Lieology—The Study of Lying

In order to be able to unmask them, we first need to look at how covert operatives maintain their pretenses. A major technique is lying. You lie when you intend to deceive someone by saying something false. When Brody tells the CIA polygraph operator that he has never been unfaithful to his wife, despite his recently having had sex with Carrie in a parking lot, he is lying ("The Good Soldier"). Also, when Brody is taking the Gettysburg tailor who made his explosive vest to a safe house, but tells his wife over the phone that he is out in his district "to reassure some union folk we haven't forgotten about them," he is lying ("State of Independence").

There are many other ways to deceive, however. For instance, you can actually deceive someone by saying something *true*. When explaining to his wife why he will be late for his speech at the dinner for wounded veterans, Brody is telling the truth when he says, "I had a flat, Jess . . . and guess what? There's no jack in the car." But he wants her to falsely conclude that the main reason for the delay is car trouble rather than his having had to chase the tailor through the woods and ultimately kill him. Of course, you can also deceive people without saying anything at all. For instance, you can plant fake evidence or you can destroy real evidence. When Brody gets his car steam-cleaned the following day in order to remove the smell of the tailor's cigarette smoke, he is trying to cover-up his murder ("New Car Smell").

Most philosophers who have studied the varieties of deception have focused on *moral* issues. For instance, Immanuel Kant argued that, while it is always wrong to lie, it can sometimes be okay to deceive people in other ways. The contemporary philosopher Jennifer Saul questions how much the method of deception really matters from a moral perspective. Along similar lines, it is not clear that killing somebody thousands of miles away by ordering a drone strike is any better than shooting him at point blank range.

Epistemologically

A few philosophers have thought about how to detect different forms of deception. For instance, with regard to verbal testimony, Hume suggests that we should "entertain a

suspicion concerning any matter of fact, when the witnesses
. . . deliver their testimony with hesitation, or on the contrary,
with too violent asseverations." And we now have more sophisticated modern techniques along the same lines. Poly-
graphs detect deception by monitoring physiological
indicators of stress, such as perspiration and increased blood
pressure.

Unfortunately, expert deceivers can beat even the polygraph. As we saw above, Brody does so when the CIA is trying to find out how Afsal Hamid got hold of the razor blade
that he used to kill himself while in custody ("The Good Soldier"). Thus, in order to defend ourselves from epistemic attacks, we need further guidance from epistemology.

Instead of just paying attention to *how* someone says
something, epistemologists suggest that we also consider
whether *what* she says (and does) hangs together with
everything else that we know. As Sherlock Holmes puts it,
"we must look for consistency. Where there is a want of it
we must suspect deception." We don't have to catch her in
a *logical* contradiction, such as saying that the barber both
shaves himself and does not shave himself. We just have to
find something that does not fit. In fact, this is how most
lies are detected. And it is how Brody discovers that Carrie
has actually had him under surveillance. During their
weekend at her family's cabin in the woods, Carrie men-
tions that *Yorkshire Gold* is Brody's favorite tea ("The
Weekend"). However, there is no good reason for her to
know that fact.

The Best Explanation of Brody

In preparation for his suicide bombing, Brody records a video
to explain why he has to kill Vice President William Walden
("Marine One"). Since the bombing does not actually take
place, the terrorists do not release the video. But it is fortu-
itously and unexpectedly recovered by Carrie and Saul in
Beirut ("Beirut is Back"). This is the "smoking gun" evidence
that finally convinces the CIA that Brody is a terrorist.

However, even without this evidence, at least three people discover that Brody is up to no good by noticing that his story does not fit the facts. The first is Carrie. While Brody notices immediately the inconsistency in what Carrie says at the cabin, Carrie later recalls an inconsistency in something that Brody had said ("Marine One"). Brody cries out Nazir's dead son's name during a dream. But if his pretenses were true, there is no reason that Brody should have known Issa. Unfortunately, Carrie only recognizes this inconsistency as she is being anesthetized to undergo electroshock therapy to treat her bipolar disorder. Since she is not able to communicate this information to anyone as she is falling asleep, and since a side effect of the therapy is memory loss, this opportunity to unmask Brody is lost.

Second, Brody's daughter also notices an important inconsistency in his behavior. Brody locks the bedroom door so that no one can come in while he is putting his explosive vest on under his dress uniform. Dana is surprised that she can't get in and asks, "Have you noticed how awkward it is, having this conversation through the door?" ("Marine One"). But it takes her a while to recognize the significance of this anomaly. At the end of the next season, when Brody is dressing for the memorial ceremony for the Vice President, Dana comes into the bedroom and says to him, "You remember that day that you were dressing in here, and you wanted me to leave? . . . It was the day that that lady came . . . You never care if I'm in here while you're getting ready" ("The Choice").

Abduction

It's not enough to simply notice that something does not fit. We ultimately want to figure out what is really going on. After she notices this inconsistency, Dana tries to figure out what would best explain the facts that she is now aware of. And she concludes that her father must be a terrorist: "And then what she said about a bomb and you wanting to hurt people . . . That the war had messed you up . . . It adds up, is the thing . . . It is the only thing that makes sense."

The official philosophical term (coined by Charles Sanders Peirce) for the type of inductive reasoning that Dana is engaging in here is "abduction." But it is more common and more enlightening to call it "inference to the best explanation." Basically, you go with the simplest story that accounts for the facts. This sort of reasoning is standard practice in science. For instance, scientists preferred Newton's theory of planetary motion to Ptolemy's theory because it provided a better explanation of the astronomical data that had been collected.

In addition to Carrie and Dana, Lauder Wakefield, who served with Brody and Walker in Iraq, also figures out that all is not as it appears to be with Brody. Lauder is suspicious of Brody throughout the series. As he tells Mike Faber, "Brody's acting weird, and he has been ever since he got back. He's not the same guy" ("New Car Smell"). Lauder even shares his suspicions with Brody himself: "How come Walker died and you came back alive? What's that about?" ("The Good Soldier"). But Lauder does finally identify a clear inconsistency in the events in which Brody has been involved.

In the final episode of the first season ("Marine One"), Walker takes three shots in an apparent attempt to assassinate the Vice President. But Walden (along with Brody and several other officials) is rushed safely into the building and into a bunker. (One of Walden's aides, Elizabeth Gaines, is the only person hit.) This leads Lauder to wonder, "What about Walker never missing a shot in his entire life, and that day, suddenly missing three?" ("Beirut Is Back"). And having noticed this inconsistency in the official story, he tries to come up with a better explanation of these events: "I'm onto Brody . . . He was on the ground that day, right? . . . When Walker shot that lady . . . They were a team . . . Maybe they were working together like old times" ("New Car Smell"). As both Lauder and Carrie correctly surmise, Brody and Walker had roles to play in the same plan. But because of the malfunction with his vest and the phone call from his daughter, Brody failed to carry out his part.

A Conspiracy!

Now, what Lauder comes up with to explain these events is a *conspiracy*. That is, he posits the existence of a group of people working together in secret to bring about a particular end. *Conspiracy theories* are often sneered at and *conspiracy theorist* is a term of derision. However, according to the contemporary philosopher David Coady, it is rational to believe a conspiracy theory if it is the best explanation available. For instance, that a group of al-Qaeda terrorists conspired to destroy the World Trade Center seems to account pretty well for what happened on 9/11. And for most of the bad things that happen in *Homeland*, a conspiracy is certainly the best explanation.

Inference to the best explanation can also be used to exonerate someone. For instance, the CIA agents ultimately conclude that Brody has *not* become a triple agent (after his visit with Nazir) because that is the best way to account for what they know. Saul remarks that "He's alive, asking us to protect his family. That's a check mark in the plus column." Also, the information that Brody gives them about Nazir's plans makes sense. As Carrie points out, "the symbolism of murdering three hundred American soldiers in front of their wives and children is quintessential Nazir."

There's a War On!

Looking for inconsistencies can be a very good strategy for detecting deception. But it is important to remember that epistemic warfare *is* a war. Deceivers will do whatever they can to make it difficult for us to notice any inconsistencies. One such method is to deceive, whenever possible, by saying something that is actually true. That way, it is much less likely that what is said will conflict with the known facts. After she kicks him out of the house for lying and keeping secrets, Jessica says that Brody can return if he tells her the truth: "I need the truth, Brody . . . And don't give me any bullshit about a bender and Billy Birkbeck" ("Q&A"). His reply,

"You're going to think this is a little crazy, Jess. I'm working for the CIA," is true, but it is deceptively far from the *whole* truth. Similarly, the terrorists do not have to doctor Brody's video in order to give a very misleading impression of who is responsible for the bombing of the memorial for the Vice President ("The Choice"). As a result of such counter-counterintelligence techniques, much more still needs to be said about how to fight and win an epistemic war. Philosophers, such as Ludlow and myself, are working on it!

13
Watching, Always Watching

CHRISTIAN COTTON

The tension between individual privacy and public security forms a leitmotif throughout *Homeland*. In the pilot episode, CIA Analyst Carrie Mathison clandestinely sets up a surveillance operation on Marine Sergeant Nicholas Brody's home to prove that Brody was "turned" while a prisoner of war in Iraq and poses an imminent threat to the United States.

Carrie is motivated by a concern for national security plus some serious feelings of personal guilt: "I *missed* something that day," Carrie tells her trusted mentor in the pilot, referring to 9/11; "I *won't* let it happen again." This quote drives all of Carrie's actions to the point of obsession, so much so she's willing to go to some pretty extreme measures, like violating the Brody family's right to privacy.

Does that sound right to you? Is the violation of an individual's right to privacy in the interests of national security morally justified? Some would say "Hell, yeah! For the good of the country? Absolutely!" But, does the good of the country *really* trump the rights of the individual? Hold that thought; there's more to the question than you may think, and it reaches to the core of our moral intuitions about what's right and what's good, and about what we ought to do in those tough cases we inevitably have to face.

Illegal, Sure, but Is It Wrong?

You may be thinking that what Carrie did was illegal, so it's wrong. But is it? The issue here isn't one of legality. We all know it's illegal (Virgil knows it and even protests, but he just can't say no to Carrie). The real question is whether it's *morally wrong,* and that's definitely a different issue. What's legal may not be moral. Slavery, after all, was legal for a very long time; but it's hard to argue that it was ever right. Sure, many people at the time may have *believed* it was; but, believing doesn't make it so, and there were many even then who believed it wasn't right. Likewise, what's moral may be illegal. Consider voting. Especially in a democratic society, voting is fundamental to the democratic process; and yet, for minorities and women, it was illegal for generations.

Carrie doesn't have sufficient evidence, legally, to suggest Brody has turned. And she knows that without probable cause she can't get a warrant. That's why she sets up the surveillance clandestinely, violating the Brody family's constitutionally protected right to privacy. But that legal right is grounded in a deeper moral insight. If what Carrie has done is wrong, it's not because it's illegal; it's because it violates people's rights.

The primary reason the Bill of Rights was added to the Constitution is that the Founders believed individuals had claims independent of government *against* the government to protect them *from* the government, not just rights granted *by* the government. So where do they come from, these rights, if they aren't granted to us by the government?

Freedom and Equality: John Locke's Theory of Natural Rights

John Locke (1632–1704) is among the most influential political philosophers of the modern period. In his *Two Treatises of Government*, he defends the claim that individuals are by nature free and equal. Living in what he calls a "state of nature," a condition prior to government, individuals have perfect freedom to act as they see fit, without asking for or relying upon anyone else's permission. And because individuals in the state of nature don't rely on the permission of others, no one has power over another, and no one is subject to another. "All men," as the saying goes, "are created equal."

Since we're naturally free and equal, no one may rightly compel us to act against our will. This is what it means to have rights. Rights are entitlements to things as well as claims against other people's interference with those things. These rights are revealed to us by what Locke calls the "law of nature," or reason. Essentially, it's as simple as recognizing that people are naturally free and equal—Thomas Jefferson did call them "self-evident truths"—and that requires that certain things be in place. Among those things to which we have rights, Locke lists life, liberty, and property. Because these rights are not man-made, they're called *natural* rights.

But what happens when we leave the state of nature and create a government? Locke maintains that we do not have a government because some people are entitled to rule over others. Instead, governments are desirable because staying in the state of nature would be inconvenient. As we move from the state of nature to government—what is called 'civil society'—some things change, but our rights do not disappear. Government has to justify its existence by defending the rights we had in a state of nature. If the government fails to continue to protect and defend those rights, we're entitled to sweep it away in a rebellion.

Now, the law of nature not only reveals these rights to us; it also teaches us that because we all have them, we shouldn't go around violating other people's rights. After all, if we're free and equal, then we ought to be treated that way. We certainly wouldn't find it okay if it happened to us. Fairness, as we call it, is one of our most basic principles, some say the very root of morality, buried deep in our evolutionary past. So: life, liberty, property—but what about a right Locke didn't mention—the right to privacy?

The Right to Privacy

There's no settled definition of privacy, much less the *right* to it, but we can still offer a reasonable definition. The right to privacy, we may say, is our right *to maintain a domain around us—including all those things that are part of us, like our bodies, our homes, our property, our identity, our thoughts, feelings, beliefs and attitudes—with the power to determine for ourselves which parts may be accessed by others and in what ways they may be accessed.*

In other words, it's the right of individuals, groups, or institutions to determine for themselves when, how, and to what extent information about them is communicated to others. Our deepest moral intuitions suggest that we ought to be free to exercise some kind of control over how information about us is accessed and used. If we believe that individuals have that kind of right to privacy, then we have to ask, lack of legal justification notwithstanding, has Carrie unjustifiably violated the Brody family's right to privacy? Another way to ask it would be: Does the good of the country trump the right of the individual?

If It's Good, Isn't It Right Too?

In order to save your country from a possible terrorist attack, you must surveil a recently returned prisoner of war whom you suspect of being a terrorist to gain intel on a possible terrorist attack in order to prevent it from happening. Does the end justify the means? Does preventing a possible attack justify the invasion of privacy? While it would certainly be *good* to prevent such an attack, it's not clear that it would be *right* to violate someone's privacy in order to do it.

All too often people confuse the notions of good and right. The confusion is understandable. Both concepts appear to apply to what we *ought to do,* and so the debate is about persuading us to act in a certain way. Should we act for the good of the country or to protect the rights of the individual? But, this is a mistake: it's only the Right that applies to *how we ought to act*, what we should do; the Good, by contrast, applies to *what we should want*, what our actions should aim to achieve.

First, we determine what we want, what goal. Carrie wants to prevent an attack on the US. Then, we have to consider the many ways we can go about realizing that goal, some of which may be inappropriate. Carrie believes that the CIA's best bet is Brody: she believes her source in Baghdad is reliable; she doesn't think the sudden emergence of Brody after eight years in the hole is a coincidence; she's convinced the best way to gather the intel is eyes and ears on the ground, and that means cameras and microphones in every corner of Brody's house. But, is that morally inappropriate?

Of course, "inappropriate" doesn't mean "ineffective"; it means "wrong" in some way. If the invasion of privacy is inappropriate, then Carrie and her crew are doing what's wrong, even if it's an effective way to achieve their ends. The *ends* we desire may be good, but the *means* we use to achieve those ends—what we do and how we do it—may be inappropriate. So, we need certain rules that tell us what means are right or appropriate. But, what's right isn't determined by what's good; something's being good doesn't make it right. The ends don't justify the means.

The Right and the Good

See, the Good has to do with benefits. If something is good, then it benefits something or someone. Think of it as giving you an advantage or being useful in achieving your purpose. This approach to ethics is called *teleological*, from the Greek word, *telos*, meaning "end," "purpose," or "goal." Because the good is defined in relation to some beneficial outcome, this approach is also called *outcomes-based*, or *consequentialist*: what is good are the consequences or outcomes of our actions. An ethic based on goodness will ask questions about the anticipated or hoped-for benefits of one course of action as opposed to another. If someone says that something's good, we can always ask "good for what?" Or . . . good for *whom*?

The Right, by contrast, has to do with principles of action. In ethical situations, we apply a moral rule to determine the right action. If an action is right, then it conforms to some rule. This approach is called *deontological*, from the Greek word, *deon*, that means "duty." According to the deontological approach, an action is justified on the basis of its conformity to a rule or principle, not based on its consequences. So, we could also call this a *rules-based* approach: what counts as a right action is one done on the basis of a moral rule. An ethic based on rightness will ask questions about which rules we ought to follow in what circumstances. And, it's morality's job to identify those rules. If someone says something's right, we can always ask "according to what rule?"

Now, we seem to have an innate sense of right and wrong, even if the actual set of rules varies from culture to culture. Whatever the variation, though, we know that some things are just not right, no matter how good the consequences. In other words, it's not always right to promote good consequences. Sometimes what's right is to do what's not optimal, and sometimes it's just wrong to do what may be best in terms of outcomes. And the deontological approach recognizes this by placing moral constraints on pursuing the good. These constraints usually take the form of categorical rules we call *rights*, like Locke's natural rights. Individual rights, then, are constraints on the pursuit of the good.

Going for the Best Outcome

John Stuart Mill (1806–1873) was the most famous and influential British moral philosopher of the nineteenth century. In his book *Utilitarianism*, Mill argues that morality is based on the principle of utility, which says that the morally right action is the one that produces the most good. So, we ought to act to maximize the good, bringing about "the greatest good for the greatest number." The first thing to notice is that this theory is outcomes-based. Right actions are understood entirely in terms of the consequences they produce. In other words, what counts as right is whatever promotes the greatest good overall.

The second thing to notice is that it's relatively easy to justify acts—ones that would normally be considered wrong—simply because they turn out to be beneficial to a greater number of people. The principle of utility, then, suggests that Carrie's actions are morally justified. It's a simple calculation: violating one man's (and his family's) right to privacy is bad; but a terrorist attack on the country is far worse. So, we have to prevent the attack, even if that means violating the rights of a few individuals. But, where do we draw the line? What if we calculated that more good could be produced by enslaving a portion of the population? This upholds the greatest good for the greatest number; but, surely this can't be right!

Mill himself is aware of this problem and calls it the "tyranny of the majority." In a later work called *On Liberty*, he argues that the sole end or purpose for which power can rightfully be exercised over individuals, against their will— that means violating their rights—is to prevent harm to others. According to this harm principle, Carrie's actions may be justified. After all, she is acting to prevent harm to others. But not so fast! What does Carrie have, really, aside from a hunch based on unverified intel? For all she knows, Brody is as squeaky clean as his poster boy patriot media makeover. This almost total lack of evidence makes it impossible to justify on moral grounds. If the CIA knew that an attack was imminent, and knew Brody was involved in some tangible way, then the harm principle would apply: they could violate his right to privacy. But, they don't.

Autonomy and Respect

As commonly understood today, autonomy is the capacity for self-determination. Being autonomous, however, isn't the same as being *respected* as an autonomous agent. To respect someone as an autonomous agent is to acknowledge that person's right to make choices and take action based on their own values and beliefs (their own conception of the Good).

A philosophical basis for treating people with respect can be found in the writings of German philosopher Immanuel Kant (1724–1804). Kant argues in his *Groundwork for the Metaphysics of Morals* that respect for persons is morally required because of our inherent worth, which he calls dignity, which comes from being rational. Rational beings use reason to make decisions about how to act and then act according to, and for the sake of, those reasons (that's what makes us *moral* agents).

Respect for persons implies an acknowledgment that they are free to act for the sake of reasons they believe are right. To treat persons with respect is to treat them as self-determining. To be self-determining is to be an "end in itself," which is a fancy way of saying something that isn't just a means to some other end. To treat people with respect, then, you must never use them merely as a means to your own or another person's ends, but always acknowledge them as an end in their own right.

According to Kant, this is one version of *the* fundamental moral principle, called the Categorical Imperative: act in such a way that you treat Humanity, whether in your own person or that of another, always as an end in itself and never merely as a means. Basically, don't use people; don't manipulate them to achieve your own (or even society's) ends, no matter how good those ends may be.

That brings us to Saul.

The Strong Arm of the Law

Saul manages (at the beginning of the episode "Grace") to get a FISA warrant—by *blackmailing* a federal judge! The basic problem here is that Saul's using *morally questionable means to secure legal justification for a morally questionable end.* He's coercing Judge Turner, violating his autonomy, to get him to issue the warrant to violate Brody's right to privacy. He blackmails a federal judge *to his face in his own office over tea after discussing art!*

This strong-arm tactic is both subtler and more repugnant than Carrie's actions. What Saul does, unlike Carrie, is openly to pursue a course of action that's morally wrong (treating Judge Turner as a mere means) to secure legal justification for the very thing we think Carrie's morally wrong to do (violating the Brodys' right to privacy for the good of the country).

The obvious tension in Saul's actions—using morally questionable means like blackmail to secure legal justification for a morally questionable end like the invasion of privacy—is clear. Remember what Saul says after Carrie tries to seduce him in her living room to "make it up" to him for lying? He said to her, very disgustedly, "What the fuck are you doing?" Oh, the irony! No, Saul: what the fuck are *you* doing?

Pursuing the Good within the Constraints of the Right

Even if it were to produce the best outcome overall, and thus be objectively doing what is best, it would nonetheless be wrong to do so: the ends do not justify the means; we should never act in such a way that we violate the autonomy, humanity, and self-determination of others, unless we know that doing so would prevent harm to others. Whatever notion of the Good we're pursuing, it must be constrained by the boundaries of the Right; we can't trample the rights of individuals (or groups) in order to secure the good for other individuals (or groups). We mustn't do wrong just because we judge that a good outcome will result.

If the Right is not morally prior to the Good, then it can be overridden or circumvented in cases where doing so appears to result in a better outcome . . . but, better for *whom*? While rights can be applied to everyone, goods may differ from one to another. Therefore, even if we say that the Good is that toward which the Right aims, just as the end is always prior to the means, so the Right must be prior to the Good, shaping the way we act to achieve it.

Things like the right to privacy, which we have conceived of as an entitlement to the control over what information about ourselves is made public, or the claim that others aren't, without our consent, entitled to that information, must then fall under the principle of autonomy, to derive from it in a sense. And it seems clear enough that a certain degree of privacy is required for genuine self-determination.

We have a right to privacy. That right is not given to us by the government but belongs to us independently of government, and it is wrong for agencies of the government to do things that invade our right to privacy, just because some government official believes that it will achieve some desirable goal, like exposing a terrorist.

VII

Critique
of Carrie's
Reason

14
Carrie's Problem of Evil

TRIP McCROSSIN

"I'm just making sure we don't get hit again," Carrie pleads with Saul, roughly two-thirds of the way through *Homeland*'s pilot episode, attempting to justify her forbidden surveillance of Brody, recently returned from eight years of captivity as a prisoner of war.

How can her actions be faulted, she insists, if her struggle is righteous, and what could be more righteous than to struggle against the evil that is terrorism, and in particular the personification of this evil in terror mastermind Nazir and his suspected recruit, Brody? Saul's concern is not with the righteousness of her struggle, also his own after all, but with her method. What Saul doesn't realize yet, but we do, is that there's a yet deeper concern, constitutional not in a legal, but in a personal sense.

In her struggle with the problem of terrorism, Carrie is struggling also with *herself*, and the burdens imposed by her own constitution, her "mood disorder," on her ability to reason through to a solution. As such, Carrie's struggle with *the problem of the evil that is terrorism* reflects a more general problem, the *problem of evil* itself, in its modern incarnation. And as *Homeland*'s overarching narrative is *about Carrie*, leading us to see ourselves in her, at least in part, we are reminded that *we* struggle with it too, and may, through her, come to understand it better.

There is much in *Homeland*'s rich and varied storyline, over the course of its first three seasons, to contribute to such an understanding. Here we make a modest beginning, by observing and developing a discernible symmetry between Carrie's understanding of herself toward the beginning of her life with Brody, as reflected in the pilot episode, and her sense of herself toward the end of it, as reflected in the third season's finale. First, though, let us develop briefly a better sense of *Homeland*'s place, and Carrie's place in particular, in the long conversation regarding the problem of evil.

The Book of Carrie

Commonly phrased as the question, "Why do bad things happen to good people, and good things to bad?," the problem of evil began its life as a theological one, as far back as the Old Testament's Book of Job, as to how we may reconcile faith in God's wisdom, power, and benevolence with the misery we regularly suffer nonetheless. Such is the spirit of the late exchange between Brody and Nassrin. Each of them devout, each struggles as such to "find peace" in the wake of their terrible suffering. For Brody, his torment is Dana's attempted suicide, having lost her "faith that her own father wouldn't betray her and make her life unliveable." Nassrin is also tormented. "Sometimes I ask," she admits, "why God had to take my son and my husband instead of me, and then I feel like your daughter did, life is unliveable." But "we survive," they agree, "it's what we do," keeping faith in spite of it all, "we crawl out of the rubble and we gather up the bodies."

But as much as Nassrin may *feel* like Dana does, her and Brody's shared faith is entirely different from what he's referring to as Dana's. In the spirit of the latter, the problem of evil is also a modern *secular* problem—as Susan Neiman has convincingly argued in her 2002 book, *Evil in Modern Thought*—posing a threat not to God's standing, but to human reason's. How can we make reasonable sense of the world, if we can't make sense of it teeming with unreasonable suffering? Whatever other problems Carrie has, she surely has this one.

Two Traditions: Rousseau versus Voltaire

The moment when the problem of evil becomes a modern *secular* problem, at the hands of Jean-Jacques Rousseau, is also the moment when the history of the problem becomes a history of two competing perspectives, reflected initially in Rousseau's very public dispute with Voltaire, from the middle of the eighteenth century, and since in their respective legacies.

Rousseau insisted perhaps most fundamentally that we are not naturally corrupt, but rather are so by our own design. "*All* is good leaving the hands of the author of things," he famously tells us at the outset of *Émile*, "but degenerates in human hands." For Rousseau, the genius of this perspective is that our redemption is in our own hands, if only we develop a new sense of ourselves, out of a new sense of the long and winding course of our corruption. Which is not to say that it's not, even for Rousseau, a complex and uncertain business ("nobody said it was going to be easy"), and only more uncertain now, it would seem, in the wake of the long run of stunning, seemingly incomprehensible atrocities since his day ("nobody said it wasn't going to get harder the longer we wait").

Perhaps we're better off following instead the lead of Rousseau's nemesis, the famous Voltaire, and his most famous character in particular, Candide, in declaring in the face of ever cleverer theories and ever more entrenched evil, that the best we can do is shrug and more narrowly "tend to our garden," as we see Carrie temporarily resolved to do, at the outset of the second season, upon her expulsion from Langley.

Redemption?

Rousseau's and Voltaire's opposing ways of responding to the problem of evil animate our intellectual history from the advent of modernity onward, which history now includes *Homeland*. Our modern anxiety regarding the correspondence between appearance and reality, an anxiety at heart of Carrie's story, is fueled by "*not* the fear that the world might not

143

turn out to be the way it seems to us . . . but rather the fear that it would," as Neiman has argued, modern responses to the problem of evil falling into two competing traditions, one beginning with Rousseau that insists that "morality demands that we make evil intelligible," the other beginning with Voltaire that insists that "morality demands that we don't."

Carrie's perspective is clearly the former, Rousseau's, and not the latter, Voltaire's. She believes in the possibility of redemption, however far gone we may be, and that it is to be found in developing a new sense of ourselves, out of a new sense of the long and winding course of our corruption. This is the possibility she offers Brody. "What do *you* want," she asks him, "what have you *always* wanted?"—precisely this, "a chance at redemption," even, as Saul describes him, as "a man who's dug himself into a hole so deep common sense would tell you there's no way out." It's the possibility that she offers even to Nazir, an even unlikelier candidate, during her captivity awaiting his play to have Brody trade Walden's life for hers. It's also the possibility that she wants for herself. She may be tempted to despair, to exile herself from the attempt, to tend to her garden. In the end, though, she's "*always* working," always "about to *solve* this fucking thing!"

Everyone's Not Me

"I missed something once before," Carrie wails, defensive in her posture, continuing her justification to Saul of the forbidden surveillance of Brody, and "I won't, I *can't*, let that happen again." "It was ten years ago," Saul answers, unmoved, "everyone missed something that day." "Yeah," Carrie answers back, memorably, "everyone's not me."

Their exchange, and this last bit of it in particular, is memorable not only for being vintage Carrie, but because as such, fans heard it again and again over the course of the first two seasons, in the background to the credits preceding all but the first and last episodes. Also, we naturally hear an echo of it in what Javadi confides toward the end of Season Three's finale, which is that "of all people" Carrie should understand that "no one is just one thing." Finally, over the course of these three seasons, following the arc of Carrie's life with Brody, from his rise from presumed dead to his public execution, it's memorable for what it reveals to us about Carrie's struggle.

We know already, by the time of her confrontation with Saul, that as a case officer Carrie is driven, if necessary to the point of defiance. When we first meet her, ten months earlier, still in Baghdad, she's on her way frantically to the prison holding an informant of hers, Hasan, who she believes has "intel about an imminent attack on US soil," on the phone pleading with Estes for an eleventh-hour intervention to prevent his execution. When Estes refuses, she defies him, bribes her way into the prison, in order to extract from him the long promised information.

We know from her exchange with Hasan that Carrie is not only driven and defiant, but also ruthless, threatening not to protect Hasan's family unless he gives up what he knows. We know that being driven, defiant, and ruthless works for her, on this occasion at least, as Hasan concedes, producing what becomes a core storyline of the first three seasons, which is that "an American prisoner of war has been turned," who Carrie comes to suspect is Brody, when she learns of his incredible rescue ten months later—for her, literally incredible. We know from her subsequent exchange with Saul, ten months later, requesting the forbidden surveillance in the first place, that Carrie's insight is typically idiosyncratic. "No one suspects a thing," she admits, "except *me*." And we know, finally, or at least suspect, that all of this is tied to a secret qualification she has for the counter-terrorism business, which is Carrie's self-described "mood disorder," which Maggie later divulges to Saul, and to us, is more specifically bipolar disorder.

What does "everyone's not me" add to this picture, of an already driven, defiant, ruthless, and idiosyncratically insightful Carrie? It's partly the phrase itself, seemingly in league with the likes of "it is what it is," "whatever happens, happens," and so on. It's partly this, but it's also the way she utters the phrase, preceded by a dismissive "yeah," at first looking away, talking as much to herself as to Saul. She betrays in this a palpable sense of resignation, to the persistence of unwelcome burden, a sense of being in this way *fated*.

We share with Carrie her sense of herself as fated, and not happily so, through the thirty-four episodes that follow, as she struggles over and over, hardship after hardship, through resistance, disappointment, disillusion, rejection, betrayal, confusion, psychosis, and worse. What Javadi admits finally to have been asking himself, is what we've been asking ourselves all along, "over and over . . . what you've gone through, the hardship, the self-abnegation . . . why, why would *anyone* do that to themselves?"

Javadi's answer is that "it was always about *him*," about Brody, "that's what you care about, maybe the only thing." We know this to be true as well. What Javadi doesn't realize, though, but we do, having listened in on Carrie and Brody struggling with one another in the safe house in Lavasan the night before, is that again there is a yet deeper reason.

No One Is Just One Thing

"I don't know what happens back home either," Carrie once again wails, again defensive in her posture, justifying to Brody now the wisdom of his recently completed mission, "what kind of life we have, or we don't have, whether it's together or apart, but there *will be* a *life*, and I'm not sorry about that, not for *one second*." The mission, Saul's invention, was for Brody to assassinate Iranian General Akbari, in an effort to resist the evil arising from, and in some sense the evil simply of dysfunctional international relations between Iran and the US. It is this for Carrie in turn, but for her it is also, and perhaps more importantly, the "chance at redemption" that she believes Brody's been seeking, which she wants for him, and wants for herself.

The mission succeeds, against all odds, eliciting a rare "well done" from Saul even, but Brody is inconsolable, his supposed redemption a "joke," he feels in the end. "In what universe," he objects, "can you redeem one murder by committing another?"

But Carrie is resolute. No matter what the cost, she's not sorry for even a second that "there *will be* a *life*" for them, as she believes still at that point there will be, "because I happen to believe that one of the reasons I was put on this Earth was for our paths to cross." Carrie's course is not only a matter of *fate*, that is, but a matter also of *providence*.

"Providence," according to Boethius's account in *The Consolation of Philosophy* (524), is

> that Divine Reason settled in the chief Governor of the World, by which he disposes of all things, but Fate or Destiny is a disposition inherent in moveable beings, by which Providence knits them together in their orders. . . . And although these things be different, yet one of them depends upon the other; for the order of Fate proceeds from the pure simplicity of Providence.

In this light, it's no wonder that Carrie adds immediately, again looking away at first, again more to herself than to Brody, "Yeah, I know how crazy that sounds." And she seems to Brody, and to us, and indeed to herself, as if she's prepared to continue on in this vein, as if there's a "but . . ." coming. After some hemming and hawing, though, to Brody's exasperated "Are you done?" she can offer only an equally exasperated "Yes." Here again, no surprise. For what more is there to say, after all, once you have taken refuge in the intersection of fate and, in its "pure simplicity," providence?

Not Crazy at All

Nor is it any wonder that she hears back from Brody, a devout Muslim, "I don't think that sounds crazy at all." We recall, for example, Brody's vision of Nazir in the moments before attempting to set off his suicide vest, reminding him that "the end of our lives is preordained; we are not created for no reason; we are only finding the path we are meant to walk on." He found a different path than Nazir had anticipated, but still he found it, and so it's the one he's meant—"put on this Earth," as Carrie would say—to walk on. That Carrie's conviction "sounds like the only sane fucking thing left to hold on to" in fact makes every sense.

And yet, Carrie *is* surprised, albeit happily so. Perhaps it's because at that moment she is thinking of Brody as *just Brody*, without thinking also of his faith. Or perhaps it's because in that moment she recognizes that her conviction *is* the conviction of a person of faith, even if *she's* not obviously such a person herself. Either way, what has to seem remarkable to us is that in the midst of discord and heartache, not to mention mortal danger, these two, one devout and one apparently secular, find that what binds them and gives them hope is *providence*.

That the crossing of their paths is providential, though, doesn't mean that their convergence will be providential, or at least that it will be the convergence that Carrie and Brody would prefer.

If He Dies . . .

Carrie's struggle with the problem of evil is nowhere more achingly portrayed than in her witnessing Brody's execution. The "good person" she has come to believe him to be, and has struggled to convince him that he is, suffers and dies without the sense of redemption they have struggled so valiantly for, all the worse given Carrie's awareness of her role in the chain of events leading to this. Without the redemption they've sought, and more specifically without Brody's conviction that he's secured it, how can his suffering and death, brought on by the struggle for this, be properly meaningful?

"The plan is a success," Javadi insists, "you and Brody pulled it off." "Not if he dies," Carrie objects, resolute in her sense that only *some* ways of being "put on this Earth" for their "paths to cross" can be right. Javadi disagrees, sadly, empathetically. "More so if he dies," he insists, as if to say that while our *feelings* would have it otherwise, surely this is the better *end* from the point of view of providence. Her choice is truly an awful one, between Brody's life and his redemption, at least as everyone other than Brody himself sees this. And we naturally expect that she'll continue to protest, to "burn it all down," as Javadi chides.

And yet she doesn't, as if to say that she sees the wisdom in his case for Brody's death. She pleads only to see him, and when Javadi insists that he's found "a kind of peace" and that she should "let that be," she retreats to requesting merely a phone call. This he grants her, reluctantly, but, after a brief moment of renewed determination at the outset, followed by meeker resistance when Brody insists, "it's over," meeker still when he adds, "I want it to be over," she finds herself finally unable to resist meaningfully when he adds, "I'm okay, I really am," except to resist his plea that she not witness his execution. She is no longer, in this moment at least, the driven, defiant, ruthless, and idiosyncratically insightful Carrie we were first introduced to, but a more broken version of herself. However broken, though, she is moved still, and self-consciously so, not only by fate, but by providence.

Her transformation is perhaps simply the acknowledgment that *in fact* "it's over." Speaking in what seems to be a purposively evocative way, he insists that "not even the almighty Saul" can prevent his execution. In anything other than resignation, he adds, "you're wasting your time," and "holding out false hope," which "doesn't help anyone." Surely, Carrie does recognize this, resigning herself to Brody's fate as a result, as she seemed already to have done, at least in part, in her conversation with Javadi. But in her final transformation we are also drawn to something deeper.

A Kind of Peace

We find Brody, before taking Carrie's call, in his cell, pouring water over himself, performing what we can't help but see as the pre-prayer cleansing ritual we've witnessed him perform before. He's preparing to pray, in advance, he must still believe, of coming soon before God. "Who Brody is," Javadi had reminded Carrie, "that is for Allah to know," and what Brody knows is that he is soon to find out.

In watching him prepare to pray, and in his final conversation with Carrie, we can't help but notice the dramatic contrast between the "kind of peace" he's clearly found, and the torment he expressed in struggling with Carrie in the safe house, inconsolable in his sense of being at that point unredeemed. "In what universe," he had protested, "can you redeem one murder by committing another," but it seems now that there *is* a universe, indeed in this very one, Brody appears to believe, in which you can be redeemed by accepting punishment for what you know to have been wrong, however tempting it may be to accept Carrie's arguments to the contrary.

Carrie's choice, between Brody's life and his redemption, is also his. In order to be redeemed, he must, by his own light, choose the latter, and in this is his "kind of peace." Carrie chooses similarly, and perhaps for her there is also, in the end, a kind of peace.

The struggle that has been their life together comes to an end in a sort of convergence after all. Brody has acted heroically, Carrie believes, and so has been redeemed in the way that she struggled for, "all the more so if he dies," as Javadi's asserted and Carrie can't help but agree. In this Brody is redeemed also, though differently, by his own light, by accepting punishment.

Taking Leave

What we learn from Carrie, then, in facing down the problem of evil so tragically in these last moments of Brody's life, is that we may meaningfully respond to it by acknowledging a providential end to things, driving our fated natures, but accepting at the same time that we have a role to play in this nonetheless, a responsibility even one might say, to craft the best and most virtuous story about ourselves that we can manage, even while the story's conclusion remains, to at least a large extent, obscure.

Brody helps her in this by finally being true to himself, by his own lights, even while aware of the pain and suffering that will come to him and to those he loves as a result. Carrie helps in this in turn, by accepting ultimately Brody's sense of himself and his fate, while being true to herself still, in acknowledging, even contrary to his wish that she not subject herself to witnessing his execution, "I have to be there," and asserting in turn, "I will be there."

And finally, in being there, she also insists, even while resigned to the fact that she can't save him, that she will help to give one last bit of meaning to his suffering, by climbing the fence, calling out his name, and only his name, drawing his gaze in the last moments of his life, and by doing so ensuring that he doesn't die alone, unacknowledged for what only Carrie, among those present, knows of him—that he is indeed, in her estimation *and* his, *and* in a way meaningfully connected with both of their suffering, a "good person."

As we see Carrie walking away from Langley's Memorial Wall, late at night four months later, having covertly inscribed Brody there as the hero she believes him to be, and believes others should believe him to be, our gaze lingers on his newly etched star. We think and feel many things, among them that in struggling with the problem of evil, in order at least to reduce the offense we feel in response to bad things happening to good people and good things to bad, it's crucial to struggle heroically, but also to recognize the heroic struggles of others, in the hope that we may ourselves model them, as we take leave for our next assignment.

15
Carrie's Personality Paradox

Frank Scalambrino

> **CARRIE:** You can't change your soul!
> **BRODY:** Yes you can.
>
> —"The Choice"

*H*omeland's Carrie Mathison is often described in terms such as "obsessive-compulsive" and "bipolar," and though she is not described as having "multiple personalities," across the first two seasons alone her identity has varied enough to make us wonder about its stability. On the one hand, we wonder about her personhood. What makes her who she is? What amount of change is sufficient to make her a different person? On the other hand, we wonder about what is often called the "personality paradox." How are we to understand the inconsistencies of someone's personality? Or, how do we understand the relation between the factors determining a person's identity and the persistence of their identity?

Carrie's Personality Paradox

A person's behavior or presentation can differ a lot depending on the situation. Playing games, acting a role, or participating in an event are all examples in which the presentations and behaviors are more or less determined by the situation, rather than by the identities of the individuals.

153

For you to be identified as a player in a game of basketball, you need to defer to the rules of the game. So, we should ask the following question about Carrie. *What ultimate factor seems to be determining Carrie's identity?*

According to Aristotle's *Metaphysics* all the different kinds of change a person can undergo may be divided into essential and non-essential change, and since a thing's essence is supposed to point to its particular substance, non-essential change is non-substantial change. For example, when you sit down or stand up, eat, sleep, think, smoke or change clothes it makes sense to say you've changed, and yet despite all these changes you essentially remain what you are, that is, human. You are essentially a particular example of the species, or type, human, and the only substantial changes possible are generation (birth) or destruction (death). Looking at it this way, as long as Carrie can be identified as a human, then she persists as essentially the same across time and change.

David Hume's response to the Aristotelian understanding of identity is twofold. First, Hume suggests that in order to understand individuals as members of a type or kind, for example, individual people as humans, *sameness* must be privileged. Consider how a person's body can change significantly from infancy to adulthood, and yet we think of the *different* bodies as being the *same* body of one person.

Second, Hume argues that types and kinds are not experienced through the senses. The information we get from the world by looking, listening, and touching can't by itself give us any idea of types or kinds. This idea must come from our own interpretation: something we add to the facts of experience.

According to Aristotle, there is something enduring about Carrie which remains independent of change. The usual candidates for such independence are soul or being. But according to Hume, Carrie's identity may depend on aspects both intrinsic and extrinsic to her. For example, Carrie's identity may depend on intrinsic factors such as her body, her knowledge or her feelings, or it may depend on extrinsic factors such as the practices in which she participates.

In the search for the ultimate factor determining Carrie's personhood, then, we can ask whether the factors we are considering are intrinsic or extrinsic to Carrie. On the one hand, despite the appearance of Carrie's instability, we may decide that her personhood ultimately remains the *same*. On the other hand, we may decide that "Carrie" is just a convenient label we use to refer to what is ultimately a number of *different* persons.

Love, Work, Religion, Soul, or Truth?

Of all the possible factors which could be discussed regarding the metaphysics of personhood or identity and persistence, the episodes of the first two seasons of *Homeland* seem mostly to suggest the following: love, work, religion, soul, and truth. Whereas we may tend to think of love and soul as intrinsic factors, we may tend to think of work and religion as extrinsic factors. Truth will be both intrinsic and extrinsic. Though these terms may be understood in different ways, they will be considered here in the way they are depicted in *Homeland*. In other words, rather than debate here what "love" is or what "truth in itself" means, we will discuss the impact and influence of the factors the *Homeland* characters refer to as love and truth. So, we're more concerned with the fact that Carrie refers to her relation to Brody as one of "love" than with the question of how to characterize that "love" abstractly.

In terms of love, recall Carrie's reaction to being confronted by Saul in Season One after he discovers she has been running an illegal surveillance of Brody. Notice how Saul's confronting Carrie can be seen as a pointing out that she has deviated from the rules in which she is supposed to be participating in order to be a CIA agent. In fact, Saul tends to continuously characterize a position which considers extrinsic factors to determine a person's identity. Yet, Carrie's initial reaction to Saul's confrontation is to show herself to Saul as a potential lover. How are we to understand this action? Is Carrie's action merely the out-of-control reaction of an unstable rogue CIA agent, or does her reaction reveal that on some level she considers participation in love to be deeper than participation in the rules which bind her and Saul as co-agents in the CIA?

In terms of work, *Homeland* is quite good at depicting the motivation for Carrie's actions as intimately covert. For example, does Carrie truly return to work with Saul at the end of Season Two to "clear" Brody's name? When Carrie is initially at her cabin with Brody, is she ultimately acting as a CIA agent attempting to obtain information from a suspected terrorist, or is she allowing herself to be in such situations with Brody because she ultimately wishes to pursue a more intimate participation? By their return to the cabin at the end of Season Two she has explicitly told us that she wants to spend her life with Brody.

In terms of religion, the question of Carrie's identity is uniquely highlighted in relation to Brody's religious conversion. At the end of Season Two Carrie explicitly says to Brody, "You can't change your soul!" To which Brody responds, "Yes you can." Philosophically this exchange is significant in that Carrie declares this at a point when she momentarily shifts from a loving to a work-related relation to Brody. She goes from looking lovingly into Brody's eyes to holding him at gunpoint. The idea that he can't change his soul, then, functions for Carrie as a kind of realization that Brody must be somehow behind the recent terrorist activity which almost killed the both of them.

Yet Brody's religious conversion has emerged in a contrasting way with his motivation to perform "terroristic" acts. This is emphasized in Season One's final episode and the tape Brody makes in which he declares that the acts he planned to perform were consistent with his identity as a US Marine, "defending America" from "domestic" enemies. Hence, Brody's response to Carrie indicates the power of religion to determine a person's identity. Brody's religious conversion allows him to see that—just like *his* soul—a soul can change, and, in fact, it is this exact change which seems to have allowed Brody (at least at this point) to no longer be motivated to perform violent acts of retribution.

Further, in terms of soul then, we can ask questions regarding Carrie's psychological state. The term "soul" works well here both because Carrie seems concerned with the idea of a person's soul and soul is a wide enough term to be used in both religious and psychological contexts. In this way, bipolar mania may be thought of as indicating the state of your soul, even if lithium is privileged over prayer as the preferred method of intervention.

Carrie's insistence that you can indeed change your soul may be seen as revealing the way Carrie understands her own, at times manic, passion—as a kind of psychological disorder. Repeatedly as her disorder is introduced in Season One, Carrie—paradoxically—relates to the inconsistency of her soul as a consistent process.

Yet if the soul can change, then a number of possibilities arise. For example, Brody's religious conversion affords him the hope and faith that Carrie has changed from their first encounter at her cabin to the later encounter. Believing the soul can change, Brody can forgive Carrie for her original presentation as undercover agent suspecting him; it is as if religion for Brody allows him to see Carrie's soul changed from its identity molded by work to an identity molded by love. This may be seen in her declaration to Brody, "I wish I could have both. You and the job," and this seems to point back to love as the factor determining and sustaining Carrie's identity.

Thinking of truth as the ultimate factor determining Carrie's identity may also seem consistent with the action from Seasons One and Two of *Homeland*. Carrie considered Brody a terrorist, and when it seemed that the truth was that he was not, then her psychological disorder—the disorder, we may say, of her soul—forced her into electro-convulsive therapy (ECT) every Monday and Thursday "for six weeks." Truth, then, seemed to be functioning both intrinsically and extrinsically in relation to the identity and the sustaining, the persistence, of Carrie's personhood. Intrinsically her desire to reveal the truth essentially stabilized and animated Carrie, and extrinsically the apparent contradiction between the truth of the situation and the truth she believed she had discovered invoked a destabilization.

Know Thy Self

Look at the following potent exchange from Season Two's final episode between Carrie and Saul.

> **CARRIE:** Station Chief . . . I have to think about it . . . You know the struggles I have . . . sometimes I think about a more balanced life.
>
> **SAUL:** This is your life . . . What's *changed*? Brody? [*emphasis added*] I thought you said your eyes were open.
>
> **CARRIE:** My eyes are open. Brody has kept every promise he has made to us. Without him we would never have rolled up Nassir or his network.
>
> **SAUL:** He's a man who put on a suicide vest Carrie. That's who he is [*his identity*] that's who he always will be.
>
> **CARRIE:** I know *everything* he is, but it's complicated.
>
> **SAUL:** No. It's crystal clear. You cannot be with him.
>
> **CARRIE:** Who are you to say that to me?
>
> **SAUL:** You can do whatever you want; an intelligence officer can't.
>
> **SAUL:** You're throwing your life away.
>
> **CARRIE:** Or maybe I'm just not giving it away to this place [*work at the CIA*].

The conversation ends with Carrie pointing out that, from the point of view of *love* as determiner of identity, Saul appears to be in despair—he seems lonely and sad. Saul responds from the point of view of *work* (and perhaps religious affiliation) that Carrie's perspective is selfish and fails to see the *truth* of their communal existential situation. That situation is, of course, existence in a time of terroristic tension to determine the religious identity—through way of life—of the global community.

It is as if Saul is accusing Carrie of privileging intrinsic truth over truth extrinsically determined. This may be a tendency for Carrie in general. On the one hand, Carrie's affirmation of her vision of the truth of the initial situation involving Brody and her reluctance to entertain his innocence resulted in a kind of de-stabilizing of the truth providing order to her soul; hence, her psychological disorder. On the other hand, Carrie's identity may be seen as re-stabilized by her love for family and second job working as an English teacher.

Such a realization would suggest that it is not the *extrinsic* rules associated with work that determine Carrie's identity as much as the love motivating her that determines her identity. Perhaps Carrie privileges the *intrinsic* truth of a situation over the extrinsic. Whereas she could cope with breaking the rules that supposedly bind her to an identity as a CIA agent, she seemed much less able to cope with disruption to intrinsic influences such as the directedness of her passionate love or the truth of the situation as it appeared to her.

When Saul calls Carrie "selfish," then, we can see this as an attempt to point to her tendency to privilege intrinsic determiners of identity over extrinsic. Further, despite what appears to us as Carrie's obvious love for her work as a CIA agent, she is apparently reluctant at the point of the above conversation with Saul to accept a promotion. Why? It may be that this scene is revealing a kind of integrity about Carrie which was, perhaps, previously more difficult to see. That is, Carrie's love for her work may be more intrinsically than extrinsically related.

A comparison of Carrie with Brody here illuminates both the integrity of Carrie's devotion to intrinsic identity determination and the difficulties which arise because of it. Brody seems to have allowed his identity to be determined by extrinsic factors such as his relations to the rules of his identity as a US Marine and his submission to the rules of his religious conversion before awakening to intrinsic determinations such as the witnessing of his own soul's change, his love for Abu Nassir's son, and his love for Carrie. In fact, we might think that it was his earlier allowance of extrinsic determiners which may have diminished his capacity to love his family, compared to the extent he is now able to love after his religious conversion.

Carrie's integrity regarding intrinsic identity determination commits her to the kind of position for which "You can't change your soul!" might be a slogan. Such a position allows for a kind of order despite change over time, especially, for example, those changes relative to politics. Carrie can maintain a kind of intrinsic integrity despite a change in the political interests and the accompanying change in rules determining her work identity as a CIA agent. Yet, the difficulties related to such a position involve a kind of intrinsic chaos and disorder when commitment to an intrinsic factor determining her identity is disrupted. Examples of this were her love for Brody and her commitment to the truth of Brody's initial identity. *Homeland* emphasized this dynamic by mirroring it in Brody's daughter's despair at not being able to confess guilt related to the drunken car accident and subsequently be re-instated in a world governed by truth and justice, rather than power and money.

The Metaphysics of Carrie's Personhood

Carrie has a tendency to determine her own identity in terms of intrinsic factors. So, Carrie seems to tend more toward love and the intrinsic truth of a situation, rather than the rules prescribed by a work or religious identity—though this is not to say that she deliberately seeks to violate these rules. We identified this tendency with Carrie as a kind of integrity. Yet, we also noted the difficulties or "struggles" Carrie experiences intimately related to such integrity.

An examination of the factors determining Saul's identity contrast with Carrie's in that Saul's seem to be ultimately extrinsic factors. Brody is a special case in the metaphysics of personhood insofar as he may have experienced a shift in factors ultimately determining his identity, from extrinsic to intrinsic. To investigate these cases further we might consider religious conversion in terms analogous to our consideration of truth and its relation to love. Just what kind of insight allowed Brody's realization that the soul can change? And, how does that insight relate extrinsically to religion and intrinsically to truth and love?

VIII

Interrogating Interrogation

16
Interrogation and Lying

ROBERT ARP

In the Season One episode "Blind Spot" Saul interrogates the recently captured Afsal Hamid, an Iraqi terrorist, mid-level member of Abu Nazir's faction, and one-time interrogator and guard of Brody when he was in captivity in Iraq. Apparently, Hamid was kind of a prick to Brody, once even urinating on him just after beating him severely.

During the videotaped interrogation, Saul tells Hamid that he'll be able to protect Hamid's family from Abu Nazir, if he's willing to give up some valuable information about Nazir, his whereabouts, and his organization. Hamid is stiff-lipped and stoic, so Saul leaves him in the interrogation room with the air conditioning on full blast, lights blinking intermittently, and the sound of loud heavy metal music. After several hours of this treatment, Hamid complies and gives up a Pakistani email address, and Saul and Carrie go off to pursue leads associated with the email.

The email does eventually lead them to shadow Raqim Faisel who's actually part of an anti-American sleeper cell. In the meantime, Brody is allowed to confront and interrogate Hamid and, after Hamid spits in Brody's face, the two fight each other in one of the room's blind spots off camera. A short time later it is discovered that Hamid has killed himself by slashing his own wrists with a piece of a razor blade, despite the fact that Carrie and others put him through a thorough cavity search. Carrie, Saul, and we the viewers are left with the impression that Brody slipped Hamid the piece of razor blade in the blind spot, probably knowing that Hamid would use it to kill himself.

Asking Questions

This episode got us to thinking about the nature and process of interrogation, as well as the dynamic interplay of truth and lies found in the relationship between the interrogator and the one interrogated, the so-called *source*. The English word 'interrogation' is derived from the Old French *interrogación* (thirteenth century) and ultimately the Latin *interrogationem*, both meaning "an asking, a question, or a questioning." The US Army's "Field Manual (FM) 34-52: Intelligence Interrogation" offers a useful and commonsense definition and description of interrogation:

> Interrogation is the art of questioning and examining a source to obtain the maximum amount of usable information. The goal of any interrogation is to obtain usable and reliable information, in a lawful manner and in the least amount of time, which meets intelligence requirements of any echelon of command. Sources may be civilian internees, insurgents, enemy prisoners of war (EPWs), defectors, refugees, displaced persons, and agents or suspected agents. A successful interrogation produces needed information which is timely, complete, clear, and accurate. An interrogation involves the interaction of two personalities: the source and the interrogator. Each contact between these two differs to some degree because of their individual characteristics and capabilities, and because the circumstances of each contact and the physical environment vary.

The US Army talks about sources as being EPWs, insurgents, defectors, agents, and the like whose information affects the security of the nation, but we all know that interrogations of suspected criminals and those people thought to be associated with criminals and crimes occur daily. Watch any episode of any of the series from the *Law & Order* franchise and you'll see at least one example of a fictional interrogation, while every episode of *The First 48* shows parts of actual videotaped interrogations related to homicides.

We Have Ways of Making You Talk

Interrogators use a variety of methods or techniques to try and get sources to deliver the goods. One that's commonly utilized has to do with fatiguing the source so as to break down the source's resistance to reveal information, thereby getting her or him to talk. There are varying degrees of this method, and many of them can be considered forms of torture. Here, we're talking about utilizing something uncomfortable to get someone to talk—not breaking bones, ripping out fingernails, or other kinds of maiming. When Saul subjected Hamid to annoying lights, cold temperatures, and loud music for several hours—probably to deprive him of sleep—this was a good example of fatiguing the source. Saul and the other interrogators "broke him down," so to speak, and Hamid talked. Sleep deprivation, food deprivation, prolonged exposure to annoying things like water torture (waterboarding, Chinese water torture, dunking), as well as electroshocking and administering a truth serum such as sodium amytal have been utilized by interrogators throughout history to induce fatigue and get folks to spill their guts. In June of 2013, for example, a judge ruled that a truth serum may be used as part of a "narcoanalytic interview" on James Holmes, the guy who had killed twelve people and injured seventy in a Colorado shooting spree at a midnight showing of *The Dark Knight Rises*.

Speaking of spilling guts, out-and-out torture is an extreme form of fatiguing that has at times included—you guessed it— literally spilling someone's guts. Watch a few episodes of *24* and chances are you'll see Jack Baur torturing someone with a knife, pair of pliers, or even a blowtorch to get information. In one episode, Baur ends up spilling someone's guts and searching through the guy's entrails to retrieve a SIM card. Check out a show on the Discovery Channel about torture devices utilized throughout history, or visit a museum that has actual torture devices (or replicas), and you'll be at once fascinated, disgusted, and depressed that someone could do something like that to another person.

Torture and even milder forms of fatiguing performed by interrogators has proven *not* to be very effective at gathering the "timely, complete, clear, and accurate" information that the US Army talks about in their Field Manual above. The email that Hamid gave up, for example, really wasn't all that valuable, and definitely wasn't a *direct* line to Raqim Faisel or to evidence of Faisel's terrorist activities. Think of the obvious fact that someone who is being tortured—or even the recipient of what would be considered a mild degree of discomfort—will often lie or simply say anything to end the pain or discomfort. How many false confessions throughout history have been obtained from people who just want to end the psychological, emotional, or physical pain of the interrogation? And how many infidels, witches, possessed people, and guilty folks who *were not in fact* infidels, witches, possessed, or guilty have chosen death as a relief from the interrogation? Countless articles and books have been published in the past fifty years by psychologists, sociologists, historians, and neurobiologists that argue for the simple fact that torture tends to make the information from the source less reliable. In his article from the 2009 edition of *Trends in Cognitive Sciences* called "Torturing the Brain: On the Folk Psychology and Folk Neurobiology Motivating 'Enhanced' and Coercive Interrogation Techniques," neuroscientist Shane O'Mara notes that "solid scientific evidence on how repeated and extreme stress and pain affect memory and executive functions (such as planning or forming intentions) suggests these techniques are unlikely to do anything other than the opposite of that intended by coercive or 'enhanced' interrogation."

Good Cop, Bad Cop

In the Season Two episode "Q & A," Brody is interrogated by Quinn about his knowledge of Abu Nazir's son and his involvement in a plot to kill Vice President Walden with a suicide vest. At one point in the interrogation, Quinn explodes at Brody and stabs him in the hand with a knife before being pulled out of the room by Saul and Carrie. "Every good cop needs a bad cop," Quinn tells Saul later, and Quinn obviously acted like a bad cop. Carrie then enters the room, shuts off all of the cameras, uncuffs Brody, and gets him some water. Guess what part Carrie is playing in the interrogation now? You guessed it. As the "good cop" she appeals to their past romantic relationship as well as his moral sensibilities and obligations as a family man to get him to confess that Abu Nazir is planning an attack on the US and give up two names of Nazir's cohorts. Carrie's being nice to Brody builds a rapport with him and that niceness seems to be at least part of the reason Brody spills the beans.

It's common knowledge nowadays that interrogators rarely use a blatant good cop, bad cop approach, even though this image is constantly portrayed on TV shows and in the movies. Still, it does occur in more subtle ways, as Richard Leo shows in his 2008 book, *Police Interrogation and American Justice*, and as various researchers have demonstrated after analyzing interrogation videos, such as those on *The First 48*. A very funny scene occurs in the movie *The Other Guys* when Will Farrell goes off on a guy he and Marky Mark Wahlberg are interrogating by throwing him down on the desk in the guy's office and tearing paintings off the walls. Afterwards, while walking outside Farrell says to Wahlberg, "I saw how aggressive you were being and I thought, 'Wow, I gotta go even bigger than that,' since we are doing bad cop, bad cop." To which Wahlberg responds, "What!? No, I said *good* cop, bad cop."

Reid-ing the Situation

John E. Reid & Associates, Inc. has developed and trademarked a method of interrogation for likely suspects of crimes that is referenced in tons of interrogation literature and actually utilized by plenty of law enforcement agencies—

explicitly or implicitly—around the world. Called the *Reid technique*, it includes the following nine steps which, if you watch enough of these *The First 48* kinds of shows with footage of actual interrogations, you'll start to see at work: 1. The Positive Confrontation, where the interrogator presents the suspect with evidence—real or fabricated—of her or his involvement in a crime; 2. Theme Development, where the interrogator shifts focus to the context of and reasons for the crime; 3. Handling Denials, where the interrogator discourages the suspect from denying involvement in the crime; 4. Overcoming Objections, where the suspect usually elaborates on reasons why they did not commit the crime; 5. Procuring and Retaining the Suspect's Attention, where the interrogator ups the ante on rapport through physical closeness and gestures of sincerity to illicit a confession; 6. Handling the Suspect's Passive Mood, where the suspect usually cries or is forlorn—probably because of guilt—and the interrogator tries to leverage this toward a confession; 7. Presenting an Alternative Question, where the interrogator offers two (or sometimes more) choices for what happened, but whichever alternative the suspect chooses, they admit guilt; 8. Detailing the Offense, where the suspect finally confesses to the crime; and 9. Elements of Oral and Written Statements, where the confession is officially documented in written, audio, or video form.

Now, the Reid technique has some problems. Step number 7. sets up an "I'm screwed either way" situation since you're guilty whichever you choose. On the Reid & Associates website, you'll find these questions: "Did you plan this thing out for months in advance, or did it just happen on the spur of the moment?" or, "Did you steal that money to buy drugs and booze, or was it used to help out your family?" But what if you really, truly didn't commit the crime? The questions are obviously a set up.

But more problematic, if an interrogator thinks that someone is guilty right off the bat and has already put together a scenario as to how the crime occurred, it obviously biases, affects, and ultimately steers the interrogation in the direction of the *interrogator's* scenario, and it may be that the scenario is fabricated and doesn't match up with what actually occurred. In other words, Detective Dan may be convinced in his own mind that Suspect Sally committed the crime, but she didn't really, and she may confess to a crime she did not commit. There are countless examples of this having occurred in real life, and when you start looking through the profiles of exonerated people helped through The Innocence Project—founded in 1992 to assist prisoners who could be proven innocent through DNA testing—you see how in several cases interrogator bias and scenario fabrication were contributing factors to the false confessions that led to unjust jail time.

Liar, Liar

Allowing the source to deceive the interrogator, and then presenting the source with evidence of the deception, is another way to get the source to talk. One thing we didn't mention above when we talked about "Q&A" is the fact that, before he stabbed him in the hand, Quinn asked Brody a set of questions and allowed Brody to lie over and over, before then showing him a video of Brody where he himself is shown contradicting himself. When Quinn returns to the interrogation room after letting Brody stew a bit, Brody confesses to knowing and caring for Nazir's son, Issa, probably because he was presented with direct evidence of his own BS. Later on, Carrie uses the "go ahead and deceive me" technique and traps Brody in a lie relating to the confession video, asking Brody further, "When the last time you told the truth about something?" Again, Brody confesses because he's been caught in a lie.

Carrie utilizes deception constantly in her interrogations as well as in most of her dealings with people as a CIA agent. Deceiving the source is yet another technique utilized by interrogators for getting the source to talk. In "Q&A" when Carrie shuts off the cameras while interrogating Brody, she wants him to think that it's an "off the record" private conversation just between the two of them, but she knows the audio is still working, and Saul and Quinn can hear what's going on while they sit in the other room. She's also probably being deceptive when she says she wishes Brody would leave his wife and family and move in with her. Saul deceived Hamid, too, during that interrogation when he said that Hamid's family was in danger; Saul knew that the CIA already had Hamid's family in a safe house.

Based upon Fred Inbau et al.'s standard text, *Criminal Interrogation and Confessions* (1986/2013) as well as the DC Court of Appeals' (D.A.S., 391 A.2d 255 / D.C. 1978) claim that "Confessions generally are not vitiated when they are obtained by deception or trickery, as long as the means employed are not calculated to obtain an untrue statement," Chicago lawyer Joe Obenberger maintains:

> The use of deception, trick, artifice, and dishonesty in interrogation is not a mere aberration or fluke that sometimes happens. It is simply routine in almost every law enforcement agency, and it remains routine because it is effective: When the suspect is talking with police, deception frequently breaks the suspect down and elicits confession . . . Because most courts take the view that deception is acceptable in custodial interrogation so long as it is not likely to elicit false statements from a suspect, it is a widely accepted practice to tell the suspect untruths about his case. He will be told that his co-arrestees have made a statement and have identified him as the ringleader, even when they have remained silent. He will be told that his fingerprints were found at the crime scene even when it is not true. None of this will make his subsequent confession involuntary and inadmissible against him at trial.

Also, in the very first step of the Reid technique we mentioned above—The Positive Confrontation—evidence of the suspect's involvement in a crime may be presented to them, whether it's true or not.

Routine and Legal, but Moral?

For the most part, the use of deception is routine and legal in police, military, and government-related interrogation rooms all over the world. But, people generally frown on deception in virtually all its forms as being immoral. Think about how you felt the last time someone lied to you. You didn't like it, we're sure. Why?

It's not an exaggeration to claim that Immanuel Kant's deontological moral theory—with its emphasis upon abiding by rational principles that have been erected and articulated based upon consistency, autonomy, respect for persons, and blind justice—as well as John Stuart Mill's utilitarian moral theory—with its emphasis upon bringing about the most non-harmful (and hence, pleasurable) and beneficial consequences to a person (or sentient being) affected by an action—have acted as the basis for practical moral decision making of every stripe since the theories were formulated in the eighteenth and nineteenth centuries. It's from Kant that the modern basis for "Thou shalt not lie, *no matter what*" and "One should *always* tell the truth, *as a matter of duty and principle*," have been formulated, while it's from Mill-inspired rule utilitarians that we derive the general rule that we ought to tell the truth, based upon the fact that lying regularly brings about detrimental consequences in almost every situation. Starting in the middle of the twentieth century, a third perspective based in Aristotle's (384–322 B.C.E.) virtue theory has become influential in moral decision making and a viable contender with the theories of Kant and Mill. From the virtue perspective, we should not lie because not only will lying make us a liar, but it also contributes to an unhealthy, imbalanced, vicious personality.

Lying for a Greater Good?

So there are solid philosophical reasons demonstrating that lies and deception are immoral based on the arguments of Kant, Mill, and Aristotle. These philosophical reasons bolster our intuitions that we friggin' hate it when someone lies to us. When you tell a typical lie, you intend to deceive someone else, usually so that you—the liar—can gain profit, pleasure, or advantage (or to avoid hassles, pain, or disadvantage) as a result of the lie and deception. No one thinks that this kind of lie can be morally justified, and people would almost assuredly avoid and shun you if you were this kind of a lying prick.

But, you can also lie to someone to avoid a perceived negative, detrimental, or painful physical or psychological consequence—or to promote a perceived positive, healthy, or pleasurable consequence—*for the person to whom you're lying*. In other words, you can lie to them for their own good. For example, let's say Carrie's sister, Maggie, dies in a horrible accident and Carrie witnessed it, and she literally knows "all of the gory details." One of Maggie's kids asks Carrie point blank, "Aunt Carrie, I know you were there when Mom died. Can you tell me exactly what you saw?" No one would think Carrie did anything wrong if she simply lied to her niece by saying something like, "I honestly don't know, honey, I blacked out . . ." or made up some other baloney story.

You can also lie to promote a positive, healthy, or pleasurable consequence *for the sake of a whole bunch of people*—for the "greater good," so to speak. So, if Saul lied to a terrorist by telling her that he'll let her go free if she reveals where she hid the bomb, and after she reveals where it's located, Saul still throws her ass in jail, hardly anyone would say, "Tsk, tsk . . . shame on you! How *dare* you lie to that terrorist!" Saul's lie just saved several lives, so most would say he was right to lie. This kind of "lying for the greater good" is precisely the basis for why it's customary and legal for interrogators to lie to suspects in interrogation rooms all over the world. The greater good is taking some jerk off the streets and making the community a little safer for everyone, and if we have to lie a bit to make this happen, then we should do it!

In fact, although above we said that Mill-inspired rule utilitarians argue that we should tell the truth *as a general rule* (that's why they're called rule utilitarians), there are situations like interrogations where the rule does not, may not, and even should not apply, especially if by deception and lies we bring about the goods. Some utilitarians even argue that we should torture suspects to get information, if necessary (and if it works, of course). You've heard of the principle that "the end justifies the means?" Well, that thinking fits squarely with utilitarian moral thinking here. If the end is bringing about justice related to a crime, then this justifies utilizing lies and deception as a means to that end.

17
Torture by Any Other Name

Dona Cayetana and Nathan Everson

Torture is one of the overriding themes of *Homeland*. The show's two leading characters, Marine Sergeant Nicholas Brody and CIA Agent Carrie Mathison, are not only tortured at some point in their fictional lives, but they also torture other people. In the very first episode of the series, for example, Brody is rescued from Afghanistan after "spending eight years in a hole" being imprisoned and tortured by terrorist leader Abu Nazir.

Since the 2004 release of the photos of US military personnel torturing and humiliating Muslim prisoners in Abu Ghraib prison, ethical questions have been raised regarding what can be justified as necessary in the mission to catch terrorists. Practices such as sleep deprivation, prolonged loud noise and bright lights, waterboarding, and humiliation of male prisoners by female interrogators have come to be known as *enhanced interrogation techniques*. The participation of female officers in these practices, such as Lynndie England at Abu Ghraib, was seen as shocking given that traditionally violent war criminals have been men.

In the context of the War on Terror, Carrie embodies the ethical dilemmas that the West faces in trying to counter terrorism. She's willing to do whatever it takes to "get her man." She deprives herself of sleep and nutrition, breaks the law, runs into life threatening situations—at home and abroad—

regularly defying her superiors, and uses her gender and sexuality in order to accomplish her mission. Brilliant and bipolar, Carrie acts as the American counterpart to Seasons One and Two's antagonist, terrorist leader Abu Nazir: they are equally driven, obsessed, unstable, and willing to go to any and all lengths to achieve their goals.

Her "tortured" personality as well as her actions in the show compel us to ask a few ethical questions: To what lengths are we willing to go to in order to stop the violent actions of terrorists? In the face of terror, are we willing to sacrifice the principles of freedom and democracy in order to protect those same principles? What role does or should torture play in securing liberty? What role does popular culture play in the normalization of torture? And what is our response to, and how are we affected by, women's active participation in torture practices?

Torture in an Age of Terror

The United Nations defines torture as

the intentional infliction of severe mental or physical pain or suffering by or with the consent of the state authorities for a specific purpose.

Torture is most often used to punish, to obtain information or a confession, to take revenge on a person or persons, or create terror and fear within a population. Some of the most common methods of physical torture include beating, electric shocks, stretching, submersion, suffocation, burns, rape, and sexual assault. Psychological forms of torture and ill treatment, which very often have the most long-lasting consequences for victims, commonly include: isolation, threats, humiliation, mock executions, mock amputations, and witnessing the torture of others. During the George W. Bush presidency (2000–2008), the use of so-called *enhanced interrogation techniques* such as hypothermia, stress positions, and waterboarding ignited public debate as to whether these methods constituted torture. Philosopher Slavoj Žižek argued that merely changing what you called something didn't change the reality of it: "Replacement of the word 'torture' with 'enhanced interrogation technique' is an extension of politically correct logic: brutal violence practiced by the state is made publicly acceptable when language is changed."

The shift in language also creates a separation between the acts perpetrated by terrorists and the retaliatory acts committed by the State. This separation creates a dichotomy between good and evil that attempts to legitimize the retaliatory actions as somehow necessary, right, just, or good. The separation is further emphasized when an enhanced interrogation technique becomes associated with a form of action carried out by the West.

As Alain Badiou argues, for example, the terms *terrorism* and *torture* are linked to the terms *Islamic*, *Muslim*, or *fundamentalist* with the victims of the terror attacks and torture being *The West*, *The Democracies*, and *America*. By contrast, the term *enhanced interrogative technique* is linked to the terms *The West*, *The Democracies*, and *America* with the objects of these techniques being *Islamic*, *Muslim*, or *fundamentalist*.

There is however nothing separating the actions performed under the guise of *enhanced interrogative techniques* from the definition of torture. Exposing a person to hypothermia, stress positions, and/or waterboarding does, in fact, inflict severe mental and physical pain and suffering on that person. To this end, *Homeland* is careful to situate the representation of US use of enhanced interrogation techniques within its portrayal of the more violent, brutal, and unjustified torture of US prisoners by Muslim extremists. While exposing the dark side of US counter-terrorism operations, it nonetheless suggests that torture practices are a necessary evil utilized as the correct means toward democratic ends in a time of terror.

Justifying the Means?

It may seem counterintuitive to some, but there are actually ethical theories out there arguing that torture is morally legitimate and a good thing as a means to get information, prevent disaster, or save lives. One such incredibly influential ethical theory is traceable back to John Stuart Mill's famous 1861 work by the same name: *utilitarianism*. A utilitarian approaches action in terms that maximize utility, with particular attention paid to maximizing happiness and reducing suffering for most people affected by a decision. What this suggests is that the moral worth of an action is determined by how the *consequences* of a particular action, rather than by one's motives or by whether one has lived up to some principle or commandment like "Thou shalt not lie."

Within a utilitarian framework, torture would be justified if it led to the consequence of reducing suffering for a number of people greater than the number of people tortured. If we can torture one person to get information about where a bomb is located so as to save the lives of a hundred people, for example, then the utilitarian says we're actually morally obligated to do it. This scenario plays out in the episode "Blind Spot" where Afsal Hamid is tortured with sporadic bursts of loud heavy metal music, cold air-conditioning, and flashing lights that cause sleep deprivation. Within a utilitarian framework this use of torture is morally legitimate and justified as the appropriate means to an end, because this torture leads to information about Raqim Faisel and Aileen Morgan who pose both an immediate and potential threat to national security.

Carrie's determination to catch Abu Nazir—by seeking information on his whereabouts or potential attacks through torture, or even lying, using people, or killing them—is driven by these utilitarian principles. Carrie suggests in the opening credits that she "missed something" that led to the attacks on 9/11 and she "can't" and "won't" let it happen again. In order to reduce the potential suffering of American citizens, the use of torture is therefore legitimized. If the greater consequence of saving the group from some evil-doer requires torturing or even killing one, two, or even a hundred people in the process, then, on utilitarian grounds, this seems morally correct.

Torture Is Never Justified

A very different approach to morals is to say that some actions are simply good or bad, *regardless of the consequences.* According to this approach, acts like murder, assault, robbery, lying, or torture are just wrong—even in those cases where they will have more good consequences than bad consequences.

This way of thinking about morality is called the *deontological* view of morality and was advocated by the famous German philosopher Immanuel Kant (1724–1804). According to Kant, people should be treated with dignity and respect at all times, under all circumstances, no matter what it is that they do, have done, want to do, or who they are—priest, prophet, counselor, king, as well as murderer, rapist, thief, or terrorist.

Followers of this deontological approach ground moral decision-making in the fact that persons are conscious, rational beings, capable of making their own free and informed decisions. A person is a kind of sanctified being who not only has an innate worth and dignity that ought to be respected, but also must always be treated as an end in himself or herself, *never* used merely as a means to some end. In other words, because they are conscious, rational beings, persons are precious in having an intrinsic value (as ends) and not an instrumental value (as a means to an end) like some object, tool, thing, or instrument.

From this perspective, morally right decisions are those decisions where a person is treated as an end, and morally wrong decisions are those where someone is treated as a mere instrument or means to an end. So, it would be immoral to use a person A as a means to further some end, goal, or purpose of another person B since, by doing so, person A is reduced to the status of a mere object or thing to be used for person B's own purposes.

The deontological claim is that torture is categorically wrong under *any* circumstances because of its intrinsic affront to human decency and dignity. Looking at the use of torture as a tool in the War on Terror from a deontological perspective, we would conclude that despite any perceived or actual threat, the use of torture not only lacks moral legitimacy in the immediate sense, but it also doesn't foster the final goals of any humanist or idealist traditions whereby humans should be constantly improving in the area of moral decency.

Torture and Popular Culture

Torture or the threat of torture has become a familiar feature of popular culture. Countless representations of police interrogations in civilian life feature such threats to the point it has become entirely taken for granted. Makers of movies and TV shows are bringing pain into the mainstream—highlighting sadism, torture, brutality, and human suffering—all in the name of entertainment. You ever watch an episode of *24*? If so, chances are that you've seen Counter Terrorist Unit bigwig, Jack Bauer, torture someone. As the depiction of violence has become mainstream, violence and torture have become embedded in our culture in ways that give them the appearance of acceptability and normalcy.

The acceptance of torture or the threat of it in many movies and TV shows about civilian life has gotten us used to torture as justified by consequences, and this leads to shows like *Homeland*, where the use of torture against terrorists and suspected terrorists on behalf of the West's War on Terror is assumed to be justified.

Torture in the *Home(land)*

In *Homeland,* Western torture practices are often more implied than represented. In contrast to real-life torture sites such as Abu Ghraib, Guantanamo Bay, and the many unknown 'black sites' that are isolated and hidden from prying eyes, in *Homeland* the traditionally safe and feminized space of the suburban home is revealed as a tortured location. We watch Carrie being watched as she uses her psychological approach to interrogate prisoners; Carrie is also shown as watching, surveying, and accessing torture and tortured bodies. Using the technique of double screening, in the first few episodes of Season One, the viewer watches Carrie watching as Brody engages in a violent sexual encounter with his wife ("Pilot"), and as he relives his tortured captivity in Iraq through his nightmares and memories that are triggered by the hounding press (Grace). These scenes not only lay the groundwork for a pattern of behavior for Carrie as a spectator of torture but also recruit the viewer to the spectacle of terror.

In the episode "Blind Spot," torture ironically takes place amid the benign domesticity of a suburban home, a so-called *safe house*. Brody is asked to participate in the interrogation because the prisoner was one of his guards while Abu Nazir was holding him captive. Brody questions Carrie directly about the nature of interrogation of Hamid. "Will he be tortured?" he asks. Carrie shakes her head and smiles, replying, "We don't do that here." Brody and Carrie then observe as Saul interrogates Hamid while Brody's background knowledge of Hamid is used to create the unequal power relation necessary to create the marketplace in which pain is withheld in exchange for information, giving the CIA the appearance of, what Saul calls, omnipotence. Even though the safety of Hamid's family is already secured, Hamid is told that if he does not reveal information they will be in danger. After the initial round of questioning Brody leaves the safe house and Hamid is then left in the interrogation room overnight to suffer aural, thermal, and visual hyper-stimulation. Carrie observes the effects of this via CCTV.

Despite Carrie's assurances to the contrary, the combined effect of enhanced interrogation techniques such as physiological and sensory stress can in fact only be described as torture. Given the season's paralleling of flashbacks to Brody's torture at the hands of Abu Nazir, and Saul's advice to Carrie to "pace herself" as she spends the night observing Hamid, the paradoxically named episode suggests that "Blind Spot" refers not only to the space off the CCTV camera where Brody is later able to slip Hamid a suicide razor, but also to an eth-ical blind spot in which we the audience, along with Carrie, not only deny we are observing torture, but also reject that certain enhanced interrogation techniques constitute torture.

Tortured Women

So how does the representation of a women participating in enhanced interrogation impact on our ethical response to these practices? While tropes of torture or the threat of tor-ture have become a common feature in popular culture as le-gitimate means to gain information, this is usually a role confined to male characters. The portrayal of Carrie Mathi-son suggests a more complex interplay of gender politics and morality at work.

First, Carrie Mathison is what Žižek calls the "new face of torture." As a pretty white woman, she draws the camera's and therefore the viewer's gaze, directing it towards the spec-tacle of terror. In *Homeland,* torture represented as en-hanced interrogation techniques, is transmuted into violent spectacle for television viewer consumption by the same media techniques that gave us the sharing of the photos of Abu Ghraib, firstly among soldiers and their families and then the wider public. Carrie, as the smart, blonde, female protagonist acts as 'white-sugar' coating to dress-up and fem-inize torture.

At the same time, Carrie's role as an active female par-ticipant in torture is presented as a problem. As we saw from the public response to the photos from Abu Ghraib (particu-larly those featuring Special Officer Lynndie England) women performing in a violent way are usually demonized. Just as the cultural expectations encoded in the terms *woman* and *terrorist* are diametrically opposed, so too do the terms *woman* and *torturer* evoke responses that attempt to explain such an anomaly by something wrong with the par-ticular person. In the War on Terror we usually assume that religious and political ideology underpins male involvement in torture practices (as in the case of Abu Nazir), while searching for personal reasons behind the actions of their female counterparts. We suppose that there must be something wrong with women who chose to act in a way so inappropriate to their gender. In *Homeland,* Carrie's patriotic fervor is driven to a large extent by personal guilt as the opening credits echo the ghosts of her failings to read the signs that pointed towards the attacks of 9/11. Not only that, but her representation as bi-polar suggests that we need the factor of mental illness as a way of explaining her seemingly gender-disordered actions.

Carrie's obsessive behavior, while gender inappropriate, is an effective enhanced interrogation technique. Her instability helps to account for her willingness to have sex with and even form an emotional connection to a man she believes is working for Al-Qaida ("The Weekend"). The revelation that she is willing to use sex as an interrogation tool if she deems it necessary even shocks Brody, as demonstrated when he confronts her at Langley saying "Fucking me to get information—is that part of the job description or do you get a promotion for showing initiative?" ("Achilles Heel").

Throughout *Homeland* Carrie's mentor, Saul Berrenson, is also not above using Carrie's instability to achieve CIA objectives. In Season Two's "Q & A," the CIA finally knows that, despite Carrie's out of control behavior, she was correct about Brody being turned by Abu Nazir. Brody rightly still claims "She's out of her mind, she's obsessed with me!" Agent Peter Quinn's interrogation methods—that include stabbing Brody in the hand with a knife—are not enough to get Brody to confess. Peter believes that Carrie is "way too emotional and reckless" to be allowed to interrogate Brody; however for Saul the physiological power of the emotionally recklessly Carrie is much too effective a tool to neglect. "You broke my heart, you know? Was that easy? Was that fun?" In asserting their connection and claiming to be the wronged party, Carrie plays on Brody's drive to protect those who love him. Carrie's perceived female vulnerability becomes an enhanced interrogation technique that she actively and effectively uses to turn Brody back to Team USA.

A Possible Moral Vacuum

In exploring the ethics of using enhanced interrogation techniques in the War on Terror, *Homeland* highlights the often ethically conflicted positions of those who claim to be protecting Western democratic principles of freedom and liberty. Carrie Mathison is the embodiment of this conflict: driven by her desire to stop another terror attack on the homeland, she violates the boundaries of ethical and gender-appropriate behavior.

We need to ask ourselves if we should enter a moral vacuum in which we sacrifice our very humanity in the fight to preserve it.

IX

Home of the Brave

18
Anything Goes?

JOHN R. FITZPATRICK

The *Homeland* universe is filled with strong characters with even stronger beliefs about the rightness of their causes and raises serious questions about war and peace in an age of terrorism.

Abu Nazir is a terrorist, and has made himself a legitimate military target. But should Walden have ordered a drone strike that resulted in the death of Nazir's son and eighty-two other children ("Marine One"), knowing that these kids would be collateral damage? And what about Abu Nazir's desire for revenge against Walden? Given the relative power differential, Nazir must fight asymmetrical warfare, but what are we to make of his elaborate plan involving the torture and breaking of Nicholas Brody and Tom Walker?

Since the modern era in philosophy (roughly 1500 to 1900) two ethical approaches have dominated in the West, deontology and utilitarianism. They start by asking the same sorts of questions. What is the right thing to do? What actions can be morally justified? But they part company when it comes time to *evaluate* actions since they have a fundamentally different answer to the question: Do the ends justify the means? And the profound differences in the way philosophers and others answer this question, are only heightened when we put it in the context of fighting just wars and fighting wars justly.

Consequences

Consequentialists say yes. They argue that the only way to evaluate means is by looking at the results. Non-consequentialists maintain that this is wrong, because some means can never be justified, no matter how satisfying or beneficial the results.

The main forms of non-consequentialisms are called deontological theories. They argue that morality limits the means that can be employed no matter what the consequences of not employing these means. Our actions are restrained by our moral duty.

In a telling sequence that unfolds over several episodes of Season One, the FBI discovers that the marine sniper, Tom Walker, has been turned, and given his skills it is imperative that he be captured or killed. The CIA operative has discovered a lead to Walker; he has been calling his ex-wife in hopes of hearing her or their child's voice. This allows the FBI to pinpoint his location and a frantic manhunt ensues. As the FBI closes in on Walker, he attempts to lose them by entering the back of a Mosque during morning prayers. Walker's plan works. As the FBI follows Walker into the unfamiliar building he avoids capture. However, as the FBI agents chase the armed and dangerous Walker, they stumble upon innocent Muslims at prayer, and in a deadly accident kill two innocent men. To avoid the obvious negative political consequences of this act, the superiors of these agents tell the press that they were being fired upon when they shot. This is completely and unequivocally false; at no point during the chase did the armed Walker fire at the agents.

After the incident, Carrie asks the agent in charge to tell the truth. "Lying is wrong," she says. You should admit that the Muslims who were killed were innocent, and not complicit in Walker's escape plan; this way their families will have no doubts about their innocence, and can be fairly compensated for their deaths. This should be done she argues, as the deontologist would suggest, simply because it is the right thing to do.

But Carrie's motives here aren't so pure. The dominant form of consequentialism is called *utilitarianism*. Although this theory is often expressed by the slogan "the greatest good for the greatest number," this slogan explains too little. The theory seems to have three main parts. First, actions are to be evaluated primarily by their consequences. Second consequences are to be judged by reference to utility, where utility is usually defined in terms of some theory of human wellbeing. Finally the utility of every individual is considered equally important. In utilitarian Jeremy Bentham's famous slogan, "Everyone counts as one and only one."

Carrie would like the FBI to come clean about the shooting, not because telling the truth is always right; after all, she even lies on several occasions to many people, including her best friend and mentor, Saul Berenson, about her bipolar mental disorder. She believes Walker escaped because he had previously been involved with the mosque. Thus, she suspects that the mosque's Imam can supply critical information that, of course, he will refuse to give.

Hiroshima and Nagasaki

A standard historical example used to illustrate the moral importance of the point that is in play here is illustrated by US President Harry Truman's decision to drop nuclear weapons on the Japanese cities Hiroshima and Nagasaki in August of 1945 so as to end World War II. As a justification for the bombings, Truman relied on the utilitarian position that it would save lives. You can even argue that it saved more Japanese lives. If an invasion of the mainland of Japan was the only reasonable alternative, the Japanese death toll could have been even more enormous. Thus, there is a utilitarian argument for the bombing without even considering the benefits to Allied troops.

The deontologist philosopher Elizabeth Anscombe thought Truman a barbaric monster. When her home university Oxford planned to grant Truman an honorary doctorate in 1956 she opposed this strenuously. "For men to choose to kill the innocent as a means to their ends," Anscombe argued "is always murder." Responding to the claim that the bombing arguably saved lives she wrote: "Come now: if you had to choose between boiling one baby and letting some frightful disaster befall a thousand people—or a million if a thousand is not enough—what would you do?"

The dilemma posed by Truman and Anscombe is a serious one because it seems to catch us on the horns of two unsatisfying choices. If your cause is just, would that justify boiling a baby? Does anything go in war? Alternatively, can we realistically expect to fight wars without killing innocent noncombatants? If not, does this require pacifism? Can force never be justified in response to German and Japanese fascism?

As a historical fact, Anscombe argued against English involvement in World War II. But President Truman would have argued that not to fight against fascism would be the greater evil. To not fight the Germans or the Japanese is to allow a greater amount of evil—to the utilitarian doing nothing *is doing something*. As the utilitarian philosopher John Stuart Mill (1806–1873) once wrote: "Let not any one pacify his conscience by the delusion that he can do no harm if he takes no part, and forms no opinion. Bad men need nothing more to compass their ends, than that good men should look on and do nothing. He is not a good man who, without a protest, allows wrong to be committed."

Thus, for the utilitarian, there is little difference between doing evil and allowing evil. But it seems this analysis leads us to Hiroshima, the firebombing of Dresden, and total war. How many innocent children would the utilitarian be willing to kill to serve the greater good? If Abu Nazir is arguably dangerous enough, William Walden's answer is simply: a lot.

Social Contract Theory

There is a long tradition in philosophy that attempts to show that this is a false dichotomy. We need not choose between *pacifism* and *total war*. There is at least one other option available. The difficulty is trying to develop a philosophically rigorous and defendable middle position between an absolutist deontology (leading to pacifism) and an anything-is-permissible-under-certain-circumstances utilitarianism (leading to total war).

For at least a thousand years Western philosophers, often working out of the Christian tradition, have struggled with both what would constitute a just reason for war, and what would constitute a just means of fighting such a war. For Christians (and Jews and Muslims too), the question of a just war is rooted in one of the Ten Commandments, "Thou Shalt Not Kill." Can one wage war without violating the commandment against killing?

One philosopher who has attempted this is John Rawls (1921–2002). Rawls is neither a deontologist nor a utilitarian. He's writing out of another enlightenment project known as *social contract theory*. Several important philosophers with quite different philosophies such as Thomas Hobbes (1588–1679), John Locke (1632–1704), Jean-Jacques Rousseau (1712–1778), and Rawls are considered social contract theorists. Their differences are legion, but what they share is a belief that morality and politics should be based on rules of conduct that rational, self-interested individuals would agree to follow if others would agree to do so as well.

What would such rules of conduct look like? Well, under just war theory both sides might rationally agree that we won't kill your non-combatants, if you agree not to kill our non-combatants. We won't kill your children, if you'll agree not to kill our children. And this line of thinking condemns both Nazir and Walden.

Justice as Fairness

Rawls' social contract theory is based on the idea that justice is fairness. What would a fair agreement look like? One example is to consider two people dividing up a cupcake. How to make a fair distribution? Well, flip a coin and ask the loser to cut the cupcake in half. The winner chooses the first piece, and the cutter takes the remaining one. If the coin toss is fair, then even the loser must agree that the distribution was fair. After all, if you got an overly small piece, it was your own fault.

When one looks at the turning of Nicholas Brody, it is clear that this reasoning is at the core of it. He's a warrior and accepts that he and other warriors are fair game. What turns him is the blatant unfairness of the death of Issa, and the killing of so many innocent children. Semper Fidelis, always faithful, is part of the Marine Corps code; the intentional killing of large numbers of children as "collateral damage," is at odds with Brody's sense of who he is. This isn't consistent with the warrior's sense of fairness.

In a moving scene from Season One's "The Vest," Brody tells his children of the heroic bayonet charge of Chamberlain's troops at the battle of Little Round Top; a critical tactical skirmish that certainly helped the Union defeat the Confederacy at Gettysburg. Out of ammunition and badly outnumbered, this approach seems suicidal, but it confused the Confederate troops, and led to a great victory. When Brody leaves a suicide note on tape, he obviously wants to be remembered as a Chamberlain, and not a terrorist.

Rational Self-Interest

Rawls developed a contractarian political theory in his well-respected work, *A Theory of Justice* (1971). Rawls argues that there are two main principles of justice that rational, self-interested people would agree to:

1. Each person has an equal right to the most extensive scheme of equal basic liberties compatible with a similar scheme of liberties for all.

2. Social and economic inequalities are to satisfy two conditions they must be (a) to the greatest benefit of the least advantaged members of society, as well as (b) attached to offices and positions open to all under conditions of fair equality of opportunity.

Why would we agree to this? Rawls asks you to put yourself in the "original position" behind a "veil of ignorance." That is, what would you agree to as a rational, self-interested person, if you did not know where you would be in "the lottery of life?" If you don't know who will be the hospital janitors or the doctors, what would be fair? Well, everyone would wish to be free, and enjoy conditions of equal liberty. Similarly, everyone would agree that if paying doctors well ensures that janitors do better than the janitors would do if doctors were paid less well, then what would be fair to the janitors is to let the doctors make the pay that maximizes the minimum pay for hospital workers. If a rising tide lifts all boats, then let the tide rise.

One might ask both Abu Nazir and William Walden to engage in the following thought experiment: Assume you knew you were going to be involved in an asymmetrical war, but had no idea which side you would be on. Would you agree to the indiscriminate killing of non-combatants? Would you agree to the use of torture on detainees? *Homeland* pushes these questions hard. If you think Brody's torture immoral, how can you justify Guantanamo Bay? If Walden was justified in the bombing of the madrassa, what made 9/11 so awful? Behind the veil of ignorance, it cannot be simply it's wrong since they did it to us.

Extreme Crisis

In a 1995 article called, "Fifty Years after Hiroshima," Rawls considers the following situation:

> Suppose that countries (states, nations) that have not previously taken prisoners of war but always have put captives to death agree by treaty to hold prisoners as slaves instead. It may be that under these conditions, since all run the risk of capture in war, this form of slavery is less unjust than present custom. This arrangement seems an advance on established institutions, if slaves are not treated too severely.

Under normal circumstances, slavery would be contrary to both of Rawl's principles of justice. Slavery violates the equality principle, since slaves have fewer rights than others. It also seems to violate the second principle, that unequal distributions of goods in a society must benefit the least fortunate. But it may be the case that if the slavery isn't overly cruel, then this change is an improvement for the least well off.

Suppose a liberal democracy was fighting a just war and lacked the resources to maintain enemy prisoners in an adequate manner. Rawls has arguments that suggest that it may be permissible to execute them. But if they could be placed in involuntary servitude for the war effort this would be an improvement. So, this could be justified, once again, as long as the conditions of involuntary servitude aren't overly cruel.

So, we can imagine the struggle against a truly unjust empire such as the Nazis might allow what the deontologist would find unthinkable, but limit it in ways that are quite different from utilitarian calculations. Writing about the necessity of defeating the fascists in World War II, Rawls argues:

> The peculiar evil of Nazism needs to be understood, since in some circumstances a democratic people might better accept defeat if the terms of peace offered were reasonable and moderate . . . and looked forward to a workable and decent political relationship. Yet characteristic of Hitler was that he accepted no possibility at all of a political relationship with his enemies.

Hitler's own generals told him he could not win the war in Russia if the Slavic peoples were reduced to serfs. Yet Hitler would not accept peace on lesser terms.

Thus, when dealing with fascists who will accept only the complete enslavement of a liberal people, there is an "extreme crisis exemption." If the only way a liberal democratic people could survive as a liberal democratic people was to violate normal rules of just war, then violating those rules might well be acceptable.

Walden and Nazir

Rawls asks: "Were there times during the war when Britain could properly have bombed Hamburg and Berlin?" His answer to this question is at the early stages of the war this would be permissible. He writes: "Yes, when Britain was alone and desperately facing Germany's superior might, moreover this period would extend until Russia had clearly beat off the first German assault in the Summer and Fall of 1941, and would be able to fight Germany to the end."

However, in the cases of the Allies' use of nuclear weapons and the fire bombings of various cities late in the war, "Neither falls under the exemption of extreme crisis. At this point the Axis powers were no longer a threat to liberal democracy in England, and they never were a threat to liberal democracy in the United States. Germany and Japan were clearly defeated states by the late stages of the war, and peace could have been achieved through less extreme means."

The question then is the following: Do Walden or Nazir find themselves in a case of "extreme crisis exemption" where the killing of innocent non-combatants could be justified? The killing of non-combatants is perhaps morally required under utilitarian considerations, and absolutely prohibited under deontological ones, but perhaps permissible under the considerations raised by Rawls.

So, here's the result: Abu Nazir is no existential threat to American democracy. So there's no justification for Walden's tactics. Similarly, the argument that Afghani life under the Taliban is unique and worthy of preservation might be interesting, but this isn't in play here; Nazir is looking for revenge.

19
Is Terrorism in the Eye of the Beholder?

WILLIAM RODRIGUEZ

Homeland centers around a US marine who has been radicalized and turned against his country by a Palestinian terrorist mastermind named Abu Nazir. The son of an expatriate engineer turned Imam living in Kuwait, Nazir becomes disenfranchised at an early age during the 1960s. In the aftermath of the Iranian revolution, Nazir becomes a jihadist, and joins forces with the mujahedeen in order to repel the Soviet invasion of Afghanistan. Over time he assumes a more active role in the al-Qaeda movement by coordinating and conducting a number of terrorist attacks against the US-led coalition.

Some may conclude that terrorism is in the eye of the beholder. After all, aren't there situations that are so unjust that the only thing to do is engage in terrorist activities? Look at the British colonists on American soil in the years leading up to the American Revolution. Nuff said. We're going to examine the justifications and the morality of terrorism as expressed by Nazir in *Homeland*. In no way do I condone the positions taken by Nazir and real life terrorists. To the contrary. This is simply an exploration of ideas and an attempt to examine the morality of terrorism as a political or military tactic.

Simple Goals

In a 2002 article called "Terrorism: Notes Toward a Definition," the late Christopher Hitchens defined terrorism as "the tactic of demanding the impossible, and demanding it at gunpoint." Although this definition is crude and demagogic, it does make an interesting point; terrorism is a tool for social and political change by small disenfranchised groups with nothing to lose. Terroristic acts can be sponsored by states to enforce political and social order, by guerrillas fighting a revolutionary cause, or by quasi-religious organizations to promote an agenda.

The goals of terrorism are simple: using force and coercion to intimidate a bigger enemy, in the process sending a symbolic message through a propagandistic violent act. There exist quite a few blurred lines when it comes to terroristic violence. One blurred line is the classification of a group as courageous freedom fighter or an organized criminal organization. Another blurred line exists regarding the message expressed between a political one or simply the attempt to justify actions that are homicidal.

Evolving Meaning

Terrorism is a difficult phenomenon to define because of the ever-evolving meaning of this term. The word *terrorism* comes from the Latin word *terrere*, to cause fear or to frighten. It came to be applied politically as a result of the reign of terror instituted by the Jacobins during the French Revolution. In this context terror was used for political reasons to curb the anarchic sentiment of the rebellion and to quash alternative claims of political power. Contrary to today's terrorism the regime of terror was systematic, organized and deliberate, an attempt to replace a corrupt political order with a new democratic political system. As Bruce Hoffman points out in his 1998 work, *Inside Terrorism*, when all was said and done over forty thousand people were executed and the term terrorism became synonymous with political abuse of power and despotism.

Historically, modern nation states have used violence, power and terroristic coercion as tools to facilitate control. Since World War II, terror has been employed as a political tool by totalitarian Marxist-Leninist regimes, by all kinds of dictatorial governments throughout the world, by colonial powers to maintain their crumbling empires, and by American foreign policy, in attempts to curb potential and imagined communist threats.

The second evolution of the term occurred as a result of nationalist revolutionary attempts in the Balkans and Armenia by those opposed to the oppressive policies of the moribund Ottoman and Hapsburg empires. The next evolutionary stage of terrorism represented "a type of covert or surrogate warfare whereby weaker states [confronted] larger more powerful rivals," as Hoffman tells us.

Finally, the term evolved to its current application in order to express the violence used by revolutionary groups to challenge the repressive measures of totalitarian regimes, or to overthrow entrenched colonial hegemonic powers. The old cliché that says that one man's terrorist is another man's freedom fighter seems relevant here. Process theologian John Cobb maintains that the problem is one of perception. Interpretations of terroristic action and the horrendous aftermath of these acts depend on who is interpreting the acts. If they are perpetrated by marginalized elements to express their grievances and discontent, they may be considered excusable. If perpetrated against innocent bystanders of the status quo, they may be deemed vicious and inexcusable.

Working Definition

Given these varying usages, a good working definition comes from Cheryl Kirk-Duggan in her 2002 article titled "Civil War, Civil Rights, World Trade Center." Terrorism is the "systematic use of terror, of intense fear and violence, to effect coercion. The violence involves injurious physical, emotional, mental, spiritual, or psychological action." Based on this definition, what horrifies us and fills us with dread, to the point that the mere word terrorism becomes anathema, is the fact that those who practice violence intentionally target civilians as well as the military.

Scholars have theorized that much of the religiously motivated violence is occasioned by a fundamentalism that is the product of challenges posed by modernity and economic changes in society from agrarian to industrial. The economic displacement and the challenge to values, institutions, meaning, and their very ways of life are manipulated and exploited by zealous extremists who seek to create a society based on their theological ideals. In his 2000 book, *Terrorism: Theirs and Ours*, Eqbal Ahmad identified four responses to the crisis created by modernity: restoring society to the old ways of life; reforming society through adaptation to modern developments; the co-optation of religion for political means; and revolutionary responses.

Fatwa and Jihad

So what are the situations and circumstances that led to Nazir's radicalization and turn to terrorism? We assume that as a top official and operational head of al-Qaeda, Nazir was aware of and in agreement with the sentiments expressed by Osama Bin Laden in the World Islamic Front's 1998 statement, *Jihad Against Jews and Crusaders*, and his response to a letter written by American scholars in 2002, *A Letter to America*.

The 1998 statement asserts a number of grievances against the US and issues a fatwa (religious decree) declaring a defensive jihad. The statement establishes three main grievances against America and its allies. Firstly, as a result of the First Gulf War, the US established a presence in Saudi Arabia, and consequently Islam's holiest sites. In addition, the US was using Saudi Arabia as a staging ground for reinforcing the destructive sanctions against Iraq. Secondly, these sanctions have had a devastating effect on innocent Iraqi civilians and have harmed over a million people. Finally, Bin Laden establishes a connection between Iraq and the Palestinian-Israeli conflict. The real goal of the American actions in Iraq, is to divert attention away from the abuses inflicted against the Palestinian people.

Abu Nazir's experience, as an oppressed Palestinian, becomes one of the motivations for his fight against America. Bin Laden and Abu Nazir also see these American actions as a war waged against Islamic religion and the *ummah* (worldwide community of Muslims). Al-Qaeda, and consequently Abu Nazir, are waging a defensive war. In the *Hadith* (the second Muslim scripture, after the Quran) the term *jihad* has two meanings. The greater *jihad*, which refers to a person's internal spiritual struggle to become a better human being; and the smaller *jihad*, which refers to bellicose acts for the purpose of defending the community and the faith. According to bin Laden, Jihadists have a religious obligation to kill Americans and their allies, expel them from the Holy sites and the lands of Islam, and to eliminate all oppression and aggression waged against Muslims.

In February 2002, a group of American scholars and intellectuals published a letter in *The Washington Post* titled "What We're Fighting For: A Letter from America." They established that under the principles of Just War theory, America was defending itself and its values that included the universal principles of freedom and equality, defending the right to human flourishing, the attainment of individual ends, and the defense of religious freedom.

Bin Laden responded in the fall of 2002, with a vitriolic diatribe reiterating why his organization was fighting America and had targeted civilians on September 11th, 2001. The grievances included those previously indicated but also included a challenge to civilian innocence and to the concept of freedom. In addition to the indignities suffered by the Palestinians at the hands of the Israelis, the US and its allies have harmed Muslims in Somalia, Chechnya, and Kashmir. The US foreign and economic policies harm Muslims and steal their wealth (and oil) on a daily basis. This foreign policy supports corrupt, murderous regimes in Muslim countries, as attested by licentious Saudi Prince Farid Bin Abbud in the show.

Bin Laden also leveled the false accusation that the US supported a Zionist plot to destroy the Al-Aqsa mosque in the city of Jerusalem. An added twist to the self-defense claim justified the targeting of civilians. He reasoned that since the American people chose their leaders, they are complicit in the actions of their government. (This justification ignores the facts that not all of the innocent casualties of the September 11th attacks were American citizens, and that many Americans voted against those who actually won election.) Besides, Americans pay taxes that fuel the war machine and subsidize the Israeli atrocities against Palestinians. Americans also make up the military that inflicts so much harm upon innocent Muslims.

Finally, in a brilliant stroke of patronizing irony, Bin Laden intimated that America's notion of freedom is contributing to Godlessness and a moral laxity that teeters on the edge of libertinism. His list of abuses is extensive. American freedoms contribute to abusive economic policies that benefit the rich and allow for obnoxious rates of usury, drug and alcohol abuse, gambling, the exploitation of women, the sex industry, creating the AIDS epidemic, the destruction of nature, a dysfunctional criminal justice system, violations of human rights around the world, and most importantly, bad manners. Once the critiques are leveled Bin Laden sets the conditions which will put an end to the mujahedeen jihad against the West. The conditions are quite simple. The US must leave Muslim countries. The US must stop supporting corrupt regimes in Muslim countries. Finally, the US must stop supporting Israel.

Utility

So what are Abu Nazir and al-Qaeda trying to accomplish? It is difficult to tell whether the terrorist attacks would cease once these conditions were met. Certainly the US presence in Saudi Arabia is no longer an issue, nor the sanctions in Iraq. Yet it appears that the threat has not diminished even after a decade of war. Some scholars have identified the real issue behind the jihad against America and the West as a clash of civilizations and the aspiration of a global dominance motivated by the religious imperative of Islamic proselytization at the point of the sword. Nevertheless, the majority of the scholarship points to an attempt on the part of jihadists to promote their political agenda through symbolic violent messages.

Regardless of their motives and their endgame, their actions beg for a moral examination and justification. For the sake of argument we'll examine the morality of terrorism using two philosophical approaches: utilitarianism and deontology.

From a utilitarian perspective, terrorism can be justified as a form of self-defense under two conditions; it must be a last resort, and it must be directed against members of a community or group which is collectively guilty of violence. Just War theory establishes that before combat is initiated all political, diplomatic, and legal remedies must be exhausted. The *jus ad bellum* criteria, principles used to justify going to war, are concerned with attempts to remedy an injustice. One of the most important criteria leading up to the criteria of "Last Resort" is "Just Cause." Self-defense and the protection of innocent life, claimed by al-Qaeda may point to a justification but other principles such as "Competent Authority" (relating to questions of legitimacy) and "Right Intention" (applying to just ends) are problematic.

The difficulty of applying these criteria to Abu Nazir's actions is that these usually apply to nation-states and not para-military organization such as al-Qaeda. We can also point out that other means to remedy these complaints were not attempted. This may seem like a ridiculous claim, and you can even counter that repeated attempts have been made to condemn Israel's treatment of the Palestinians in the United Nations, but it seems clear that other means could have been sought.

Terroristic acts must be directed at members of a community or group that is collectively guilty of violence. A classic example would be those individuals who supported the Nazi genocide during the Second World War. In a country such the US, where much of the policy decisions made my our government run counter to the wishes and desires of the electorate, and may even be motivated by unaccountable interest groups, it is hard to accuse Americans of complicity. As stated earlier, many of the innocent victims of terrorist attacks may not be American, may not have voted for the President who implemented the unpopular policy measure, and may even be of the same religious tradition of the perpetrators of violence.

Combatants are subject to constraints. One of the most important factors in waging war is that combatants discriminate between military and civilian targets and not engage in wanton indiscriminant violence. In effect, they are limited in the target to be attacked, the scope of the operation, and the proportion of violence to be used. Terroristic acts can be directed at noncombatants only if they are perpetrators or accomplices guilty of initiating and participating in violence. This may not be true for the victims of al-Qaeda. Looked at in this way, it appears that Abu Nazir's actions cannot be morally justified.

Deontology

From a deontological perspective, terrorism, in all of its types and forms is always wrong because it always violates two important principles of Just War Theory, the principle of discrimination and the principle of proportion, and is a violation of human rights. Here, it's absolutely necessary for combatants to discriminate between military and non-military targets. Civilians can *never* be targeted. This is problematic in cases of guerrilla warfare or in cases of revolt since civilians are targeted because of collective guilt or culpability by association.

To complicate matters more, terrorists broaden the category to include others who are indirectly responsible or may even constitute bystanders who are in the wrong place at the wrong time. For example, in 1997 Ayman al-Zawahiri's group Egyptian Islamic Jihad murdered and mutilated fifty-eight tourists at the temple of Luxor in order to protest the abuses of the Egyptian government. A recent attack by a Sinai-based Al-Qaeda group killed three South Korean tourists in Israel (February 16th, 2014). The justifications for these murder of innocent bystanders in both cases is that tourists are contributing to the economy of Egypt and Israel.

The principle of proportionality establishes the legitimate and proportional use of force. This principle is intended to limit the number of casualties and the cases of collateral damage. The intention is to limit both yours and your adversary's damages. It is clear that the damage caused by terrorist acts, such as the obliteration of the Twin Towers using planes as weapons of mass destruction was calculated, disproportionate and deliberate.

The International Human Rights declaration identifies the right to life as a fundamental right. Deontologists believe that this right to life includes the requirement to treat persons with dignity, and to respect their right to self-actualization and well-being. It is obvious that these values can only be performed if a person is alive. It is also clear that murdering people robs them of their autonomy and dignity as persons. Terrorism not only threatens a life, it is also a violation of a person's dignity. The harm inflicted on innocent people can never be justified.

Murderers

After a careful examination we must conclude that Abu Nazir's and Bin Laden's actions cannot be morally justified. Not only do these actions violate human rights and established conventions of war, their actions violate the principles of Islamic law as well by targeting civilians. This leads to a sobering inference: while attacks on military targets may be justified, attacks on innocent civilians are never justified. The targeting of civilians is murder. Murderers like the fictional Abu Nazir, and the all too real Osama Bin Laden were held accountable for their crimes and paid with their lives.

20
America Akbar!

ROBERTO SIRVENT AND IAN DIORIO

Homeland is a series about amnesia, discovery, conversion, and suspicion. There is a relationship between amnesia and killing for the nation-state. Both are products of blindness. In one case, blindness to our own memories and history. In another, blindness to the reasons why a temporal state requires from some of its citizens extraordinary acts of violence so it can maintain its creed of freedom.

Homeland is, in a way, based on a true story. Not in the sense that it is based on actual historical events. Rather, the show is true because of what it tells us about our selves, our nation, and the myths we live by. It points out some of America's hidden ideologies and fears about the nature of our democracy and the underpinnings of our religious devotion to the United States of America.

Homeland is also a pop culture product that helps us push aside—or at least question—the utopian ideology of America. It invites us to push aside the idealization of America in all its precious promise. It questions the myth of America as the perennial home of democracy. It reminds us that the Unites States is home to a history of oppression, violence, and homegrown terrorism. Some citizens of America have only recently become benefactors of America's constitutional promise, revealing how some promises take time to go from fiction to truth.

For *Homeland*, the "city on a hill" that is America does not convince all who are born within its borders that it is home to the only hope in the world. America is fragile. One can forget this because Americans are so ready to kill and surrender their children unto death for the hope of America. It is this violence that is used to cover over the fragility of a nation. *Homeland* therefore bears witness to another hidden history: the common occurrence of those who have killed and been wounded for the state.

Killing for What, Exactly?

Is the nation-state worth killing for? A typical response to this question may go something like this: "Of course the nation-state is worth protecting. Isn't dying for our fellow men and women a heroic and virtuous act? And isn't killing, while far from ideal, a morally permissible act in cases of self-defense?"

The knee-jerk response to our question assumes that dying for the nation-state is the same thing as dying for the people who live *in* the nation-state. Carrie appears to share this view during a bedside conversation with her niece in the episode "Achilles Heel." "You should come live with us," her niece says. "We'll protect you." Carrie, wearing the hat of loving aunt and loving bureaucrat, replies, "No, that's *my* job." And with that she seemingly convinces herself, her family, and the viewer that the CIA exists to protect us from our enemies. How noble, right?

Not so fast. This position ignores the fact that the United States created these enemies in the first place. The nation-state's violence doesn't *protect* it from its enemies as much as it *provokes* them. As the episode "Gerontion" reminds us, acts committed in the name of national security rarely make us more secure. Here we find an FBI agent interrogating Quinn about the bloodbath that took place in the home of two innocent women. The agent, like most viewers at home, is fed up with the CIA justifying such massacres in the name of national security. "Fucking people," he says. "Have you ever done anything but makes things worse?"

So are Carrie and the rest of her team protecting *us* or *it*? In other words, are they protecting *people* or an *idea*? Some would say—especially in our post-9/11 era—that what Americans die for is the citizens of democracy rather than the idea of democracy itself. Certainly, for some this is the case. A pure form of political martyrdom does live among some people who are willing to die for their nation. To criticize dying for your nation does not deny the virtue of offering one's life up for another person. This is a pure form of love. But does dying for the nation mean the same thing as dying for the people who *live in* the nation? Often, that is what we think is going on, or perhaps even hope is going on. But is this the whole picture?

Consider the language evoked by public officials. Why, for example, do they constantly speak of preventing the next attack on *America*? And why do soldiers zealously declare their love for, yes, *America*? While *America* certainly includes those of us who live in the United States, the word also involves a lot more than that. America also consists of things like arbitrarily drawn borders and abstract ideas like freedom and democracy.

Even a quick glance at history shows that Americans have justified violence to protect their democracy, even to the degree that all actions (including the most undemocratic ones) are appropriate if used to defend it. Democracy then is not firm. It is both malleable and vulnerable. Torture, drone attacks, hiding and even denying information to the populace can be used to protect and sustain democracy as the light of the world. Aristotle (384–322 B.C.E.) famously described democracy as the tyranny of the masses.

A modern democracy like the United States shows that democracy is not the ruling will of the people. It is the ruling ideology of those in power, who through their democratic speech are able to pledge war and surrender its youth to death, not for the masses, but to protect the interest of the few. *Homeland* disrupts our blind devotion to "mass democracy" not by offering us totalitarianism in its place, but by showing us how a soldier of a democratic state can reject the freedom for which he was called upon to kill and die for.

The Cost of Doing Business?

But isn't this willingness to sacrifice just part of the social contract? Isn't it what we've all signed up for by making America our home? While Thomas Hobbes (1588–1679) and John Locke (1632–1704) have different variations of what this contract looks like, the gist of it goes like this: there is an implicit contract between me and my country. I get my rights, access to roads, fire trucks, the post office, and all that other fun stuff. In return, I promise to pay my taxes and follow the laws.

But does the contract also expect me to die and kill for it? Social contract theory assumes that behind every social institution live rational, calculating animals that are enabled by nature to make wise decisions about social relationships. They are able to 'take a step back' and look at the situation rationally and objectively. Dying for the nation-state under the guise of social contract theory implies a form of knowledge among the soldier that enables her sacrifice. The perfect citizen and soldier is one who understands the social or ideological goods for which they fight, kill, and die. If this were the true nature of things for the masses, then it might very well justify dying for the nation-state.

Yet at least one big problem stands out. In our world, how do we fully know the nature of the state for which we fight and the truth of the claims that call forth such human sacrifice? We are not given to a state of pure nature as the founders of social contract theory have proposed. Rather, we're born—or as Martin Heidegger (1889–1976) would say, *thrown*—into a world which is already a pile of human suffering and wreckage. It is not the pure state of democracy that soldiers are called on to die for, but for the *wreckage* of democracy. This is why the fragility of democracy is used to call forth its defense. It's because democracy is so fragile that citizens are cultivated to die for it. But is their sacrifice grounded in social contract theory? Do we really believe that every soldier is so grounded in a philosophical tradition that their willingness to die is a willingness to show that Hobbes and Locke were correct over Aristotle and Heidegger?

This is not to say those who are raised to kill and die for democracy are ignorant. Rather, it is to say that the intellectual training of those willing to die is formed by lines of thought which make their lives secondary to the thriving of a global good like democracy. In this sense, the democratic call to die is highly totalitarian. The nation-state, like a dictator, demands its citizenry's *total* submission. And because there is a fear underlying this sacrifice—a fear pointed out by *Homeland* itself—the death of the soldier must take on special status. The nation and the one who dies for it must find a way to make their witness *sacred*.

Protecting the Sacred

The traditional understanding of the sacred is that it reflects the special, or even sacramental nature of some thing. Mircea Eliade (1907–1986) wrote that the sacred is that which is the "opposite of the profane." Simply that which is not sacred is irrefutably profane, vulgar, and common. Sacred means we observe the world with a set of lenses that sees, and expects to see, more than meets the eye. Profane means all things are common. Recognizing this, the nation-state evokes certain rhetoric, rituals, and practices in order to present itself as sacred.

As one legal philosopher notes, "In a crisis, it remains true today that the secular state does not hesitate to speak of sacrifice, patriotism, nationalism, and homeland in the language of the sacred. The state's territory becomes consecrated ground, its history a sacred duty to maintain, its flag something to die for."

Devotion to the state is not obvious, but requires finely tuned words that call forth an emotive response. *Homeland* is full of instances where public officials employ this kind of language. For example, consider how the concepts of faith and love are used interchangeably in the interrogation scene between Saul and Al Sahrani ("Representative Brody"). "You don't believe in radical Islam," Saul says. "You love the West." Notice the salvific nature of the state and the religious response it engenders. Saul's statement pits devotion to America as an alternative to devotion to Allah. The attitude is the same, but the object is different. Allah is not worthy of your worship, Saul insists, but America certainly is. So, to *believe in* something does not mean some sort of rational assent to a doctrine or creed. Rather, it's a matter of love, loyalty, and ultimate devotion.

Even the show's short title—*Homeland*—embodies a kind of simplicity and exclusivity. Not only is the show simply and exclusively about the homeland. The lives of Carrie, Saul, and the rest of their team are simply and exclusively about the homeland, too. It's the object for which everything is sacrificed. Even the brave men and women sent to war are expected to share this devotion. In his suicide video, Brody claims that, contrary to what others might think, he loves his country. "What I am is a marine, like my father before me, and his father before him. And as a marine I swore an oath to defend the United States of America against enemies both foreign and domestic" ("Marine One").

Marines don't make promises. They *swear oaths*. For the marines, an oath to protect the homeland holds far greater weight than a mere promise. An oath calls upon something sacred, not trivial or common. It involves a pledge to protect and to be faithful to the homeland. It's right there in the official motto of the United States Marine Corps: *semper fidelis*, which, translated from Latin, means "always faithful."

Symbols and rituals also play an important role in shaping the sacred. Our country's veneration of the American flag is a great example and is captured brilliantly in the episode "The Smile," where Jessica finds out that Brody is a Muslim. As a shouting match ensues in the basement, we see Jessica frantically opening cabinets and drawers. "I don't understand," she says. "These are the people who tortured you. These are the people who if they found out Dana and Xander were having sex, they would stone her to death in a soccer stadium!" In a fit of rage, Jessica then throws his Quran on the ground. "That's not supposed to touch the floor!" Brody exclaims. Jessica pauses, obviously shocked by what Islam has done to him, and replies, "Did you actually just say that?"

But later in the episode Jessica's initial response proves to be quite ironic. In the final scene, we find Brody following Islamic tradition by giving a proper burial to his desecrated Quran. If the viewer is like Jessica, she's shocked that someone would treat a silly book in a way that reeks of religious lunacy. Not only is the Quran not supposed to touch the ground, we find out, but it also requires a proper burial.

Silly religious people, right? Maybe. But isn't this exactly how we treat the American flag? Don't the same rules and rituals of desecration and burial apply to the red, white, and blue? Aren't we told that the flag is not supposed to touch the ground? Do we not give the flag its own proper burial for a whole host of reasons? And do we not regularly pledge allegiance to it? Of course we do, because it isn't the soil that soldiers fight for but the flag. The stars on the flag function as a new constellation which points to the sacred and ultimate value of Western-style democracy. Therefore war, like the war on terrorism, is at its purest a war against an idea, and because ideas are infinite, wars against terrorism earn eternal status. A war against terrorism can go on forever because we can constantly redefine and inscribe new classes of people as the terrorist.

Dying for the Telephone Company

We expect to find rituals and worship in church. But political liturgies abound, too. America has its saints (the founding fathers), shrines (Independence Hall, Vietnam Memorial), relics (Liberty Bell), martyrs (Lincoln, fallen soldiers), inquisitions (school boards and courts enforcing patriotism), and religious festivals (Fourth of July, Flag Day). This leads political philosopher Alasdair MacIntyre to accuse the nation-state of presenting itself as both a "bureaucratic supplier of goods and services" and "a repository of sacred values, which from time to time invites one to lay down one's life on its behalf."

For MacIntyre, killing for the nation-state is the same as killing for the telephone company. This might sound like a crude association, but underneath the jarring language lives a compelling argument. The telephone company and the nation-state are similar in their finite natures. They have human inventors, proprietors, and benefactors. Their origins are man-made and so are their practices. The state is artificial and so is the telephone company. To treat the state as sacred is to apply eternal status to a temporal institution.

Why, then, do public officials employ language, rituals, and practices that we commonly associate with religion? These liturgies do not serve some merely poetic function. Rather, they are necessary if the nation-state is going to justify its strict claim on its citizens—the claim to life itself. The nation can't just point to the useful goods and services that it provides. This would place it on the same level as the telephone company. The nation-state must present itself as something more, something *divine*. Otherwise, it's going to have a tough time convincing people to die for it.

Homeland or Holy Land?

Soldiers like Nick Brody and Tom Walker are called upon to die, not to defend a temporal nation, but as Augustine (354–430) noted, a *civitas dei*, the city of God. The eternal city of America is chosen by God, so the rhetoric goes, to export the purest, eternal idea: liberal democracy. It is this sacred idea that calls forth from the heavens to willing martyrs.

What this amounts to is a unique form of political theology. It is not, as most political theologies are, a call for the secular to yield to a particular church. Rather, it's coming to terms with the idea that the nation-state is not the secular institution that it claims to be. Secularism's attempt to privatize religion has not led to religion's demise. It has allowed secular governments and ideologies to take on divine status. Or, as one author puts it, the holy has "migrated" from the church to the state. If true, perhaps the greatest form of religious devotion known on the globe today is not to Christianity or Islam, but to the American flag and the political abstractions its colors and stars point to.

Homeland challenges American ideological power because one of its own patriots has exchanged the practice of democracy, so it seems, for theocracy. To be a Muslim is to have devotion to God over and above the temporal borders of nations. This is why Islam terrifies the Western, secular, democratic nations, precisely because it does not assume that all perfect justice, love, and hope is found within any constitution. It is found in the Quran and the eternal God, greatly to be praised. The Quran transcends borders and therefore places an eternal claim on its followers, calling forth devotion that immediately structures all of life's commitments based on the superiority of God over above all national creeds.

This seems to be what frightens the West about Islam. It has a creed above the American credo. *Homeland* reveals this anxiety because it tells the story of a warrior of Western democracy who now prays Allahu Akbar, not God bless America.

Terrorism in the Homeland

Many voices were at the same time heard encouraging the executioners. They seemed reanimated themselves, in seizing with violence the most virtuous of Kings, they dragged him under the axe of the guillotine, which with one stroke severed his head from his body. All this passed in a moment. The youngest of the guards, who seemed about eighteen, immediately seized the head, and showed it to the people as he walked round the scaffold; he accompanied this monstrous ceremony with the most atrocious and indecent gestures. At first an awful silence prevailed; at length some cries of "*Vive la Republique!*" were heard. By degrees the voices multiplied and in less than ten minutes this cry, a thousand times repeated, became the universal shout of the multitude, and every hat was in the air.

We've all heard of France's Reign of Terror (1793–1794) during the French Revolution, where King Louis XVI, Marie Antoinette, and some 16,000 other royalists and monarchists lost their heads to the guillotine. Above is an account of the last moments of Louis XVI's life, as told by the minister who accompanied him to the scaffold, Henry Essex Edgeworth. *La Terreur*, as the Reign of Terror was known in French, was *terr*-ible primarily because the revolutionaries witch-hunted and executed anyone who didn't buy into their beliefs. One of the most important revolutionaries during this time, Robespierre (1758–1794), noted simply that the Revolution "owes nothing to the Enemies of the People but death" and "terror is nothing other than justice that is prompt, severe, and inflexible." The Committee of Public Safety agents that enforced the Robespierre-fueled policies of *La Terreur* by chopping people's heads off were referred to as *les terroristes*, the terrorists. Interestingly and ironically enough, Robespierre got a taste of his own medicine and would lose his head to the guillotine in 1794 at the end of *La Terreur*. The author of an article from January 30th 1795 in London's *The Times* used the word *Terrorism* to label the ideology behind the French revolutionaries, and the word began to be recorded in English-language dictionaries in 1798 as meaning the "systematic use of terror as a policy" by the government of some State.

During the French Revolution and afterward, then, terrorism was associated with the government of a State imposing its policies on the people—the State was *le terroriste*. The SS Guard (*Schützstaffel*) in Nazi Germany (1933–1945) and the Red Army in Mao Zedong's People's Republic of China (1949–1976) are clear examples of the State terrorizing detractors with the use of murder, imprisonment, and systematic lies. Beginning in the latter half of the nineteenth century, the term pulled a one-eighty and began to refer to the actions and ideologies of non-State organizations that felt that they were being unjustly treated by the State, or wanted to get rid of the State altogether, as in anarchist movements—the Enemy of the State was now *le terroriste*. The Russian anarchist, Sergei Nechayev, used the word террористических, or *terrorist*, to describe himself and the activities of his Russian faction, People's Retribution, back in 1869. "The Revolutionist is a doomed man," Nechayev noted in his *Catechism of the Revolutionist* (1869):

> He has no private interests, no affairs, sentiments, ties, property nor even a name of his own. His entire being is devoured by one purpose, one thought, one passion—the revolution. Heart and soul, not merely by word but by deed, he has severed every link with the social order and with the entire civilized world; with the

laws, good manners, conventions, and morality of that world. He is its merciless enemy and continues to inhabit it with only one purpose—to destroy it.

What about terrorism today? Deriving from the Latin *terrere* meaning "to fill with fear or dread" or "to frighten," terrorism is a concept that has been defined in multiple ways, and like many politically charged concepts there is no universal definition upon which all can agree. Still, we can point to features that are indicative of terrorism. Terrorism is an act that is:

1. *Violent, by causing bodily harm or death to the intended target that the terrorist believes deserves it.*

Think of any standard politically motivated assassination of a president or world leader. In fact, the US just remembered the fiftieth anniversary of the assassination of President John Fitzgerald Kennedy by the professed communist Lee Harvey Oswald in November of 1963.

2. *Destructive of physical infrastructure (roads, airports, dams, bridges, buildings) and/or disruptive of public services (water, electricity, trade).*

Nelson Mandela died in 2013, and he was a founding member of Umkhonto we Sizwe, a South African anti-Apartheid terrorist organization that, in the early 1960s, utilized sabotage against the South African government by bombing military installations, power plants, telephone lines, and transport links at night, when civilians were not present, so as to produce the least amount of casualties. By the mid-1980s, while Mandela was in prison, members of Umkhonto we Sizwe were bombing public places.

3. *Indiscriminate in causing bodily harm or death, despite the focus on the intended targets.*

Innocent persons are often harmed or killed in the terrorist act, and usually the terrorist knows this but figures these people are simply collateral damage. Many innocents were killed or maimed as a result of the Umkhonto we Sizwe bombings of the 1980s. Consider, too, all those who died in the Twin Towers of the World Trade Center in New York City on 9/11/01.

4. *Perpetrated in such a way as to cause psychological trauma to those who survive or witness the violence first-hand, or are privy to the effects of the violence through (a) experiencing the aftermath of the violence, (b) word-of-mouth, or (c) media sources.*

A terrorist act is orchestrated so as to have a threatening and frightening psychological effect beyond the immediate target. This causes a "we don't know when it's coming, but it's coming" kind of terror. So, beside the immediate terror associated with the terrorist activity, it's also the terror that is burned into people's memories, as well as the terror that haunts the various scenarios that people can imagine taking place at some future time.

5. *Intended to bring public, media attention to some (usually smaller) group, organization, cause, ideology, or individual that usually perceives itself as being oppressed or treated unjustly by the dominant, more powerful group, cause, ideology, or individuals that comprise the social situation in which the groups inhabit.*

Of his anarchist and terrorist activities, Mikhail Alexandrovich Bakunin (1814–1876) noted: "We must spread our principles, not with words but with deeds, for this is the most popular, the most potent, and the most irresistible form of propaganda . . . for then all will remember."

6. *Intended also by the oppressed group to create a change in the concrete policies, laws, or rules of the dominant, more powerful group toward the smaller group.*

This was clearly the intent of Umkhonto we Sizwe and other terrorist groups in South Africa during Apartheid, the system of racial segregation set up by the white ruling Afrikaner government that denied rights and privileges to the so-called black, coloured, and Indian peoples (basically, the rest of the people in South Africa) from 1948 to 1994.

7. *In line with the previous points, usually committed by some non-State or non-Government entity (person, group, organization) against some State or Government.*

Again, Umkhonto we Sizwe comes to mind, but al-Qaeda, al Shabaab, Hamas, Hezbollah, the Irish Republican Army, the Tamil Tigers, and the Taliban all have committed acts of terrorism against various governments.

The above characterization of terrorism comports well with the United Nations Secretary General report from 2004 which describes terrorism as any act "intended to cause death or serious bodily harm to civilians or non-combatants with the purpose of intimidating a population or compelling a government or an international organization to do or abstain from doing any act."

Examples of terrorist acts include assassinations, bombings, sabotage on a grand scale, kidnapping, and hijacking of airplanes or facilities. Most everyone on the planet is aware of the fact that four planes were hijacked by members of al-Qaeda in the US on the morning of September 11th 2001, with two out of Boston eventually being flown into the Twin Towers of the World Trade Center, one out of New York being flown into the side of the Pentagon, and one out of Washington, DC (United Flight 93) crashing in a field in Shanksville, Pennsylvania, after passengers tried to take the plane back. The 9/11 attacks resulted in the deaths of 2,996 people, including the 2,977 victims and the 19 hijackers. The Sunni militant Islamist and founder of al-Qaeda, Osama Bin Laden, eventually claimed responsibility for ordering and orchestrating the attacks. While inspecting images of the 1982 Israeli invasion of Lebanon in which towers and buildings in Beirut were destroyed in the siege of the capital, Bin Laden got the idea to destroy the Twin Towers, as he notes in a videotaped speech that surfaced in 2004: "While I was looking at these destroyed towers in Lebanon, it sparked in my mind that the tyrant should be punished with the same and that we should destroy towers in America, so that it tastes what we taste and would be deterred from killing our children and women."

Below are several terrorist acts perpetrated on American soil that many people might not be aware of.

One Person's Terrorist is Another Person's Patriot?

News Report: New Act of Terrorism

A local militia, believed to be a terrorist organization, attacked the property of private citizens today at our nation's busiest port. Although no one was injured in the attack, a large quantity of merchandise, considered to be valuable to its owners and loathsome to the perpetrators, was destroyed. The terrorists, dressed in disguise and apparently intoxicated, were able to escape into the night with the help of local citizens who harbor these fugitives and conceal their identities from the authorities. It is believed that the terrorist attack was a response to the policies enacted by the occupying country's government. Even stronger policies are anticipated by the local citizens.

Sound familiar? It should to US ears, since it's supposed to be a made-up report about the Boston Tea Party (December 16th 1773), the event that supposedly sparked the American Revolutionary War. Public school teachers in Texas were instructed through their 2012 curriculum and lesson plans to read the News Report aloud to students, and afterward reveal the similarities between it and the Boston Tea Party. This caused a lot of controversy, apparently, since American revolutionaries sure as hell weren't terrorists, right? Some

224

have argued, however, that this protest might be considered an act of terrorism, since it was property sabotage designed to bring wide attention to the political objectives of a non-State group, the American colonists. "What's the Boston Tea Party," you may ask? The Boston Tea Party has its roots in the Tea Act of 1773, which gave the financially struggling British East India Company the right to sell tea to the American colonies without paying taxes to the British government. American colonial merchants, however, *did* have to pay taxes on tea arriving in their ports, so they were obviously pissed, especially when they had no representation in the British government—hence, the famous rallying cry, "No taxation without representation!" In response to the Tea Act—as well as the Sugar Act (1764), Stamp Act (1765), Townsend Acts (1767), and Boston Massacre (1770)—on the night of December 16th 1773 a group of some 150 American colonists in favor of independence called the Sons of Liberty dressed up like Mohawk tribe members, boarded three ships in Boston Harbor (the *Dartmouth*, *Eleanor*, and *Beaver*) containing caskets of the British East India Company's tea, hacked open all of the 340-something tea caskets with tomahawks, axes, and clubs, and threw all of it into the Boston Harbor. Now, you know this really pissed off the British, given their love of a "spot of tea."

The Ku Klux Klan

In his book from 1885, *Three Decades of Federal Legislation, 1855 to 1885: Personal and Historical Memories of Events Preceding, During, and Since the American Civil War*, historian Samuel Cox wrote:

> In March 1870, at about eleven o'clock at night, a band of disguised men, estimated at twenty-five in number, rode into the town of Eutaw, Alabama. They formed in front of the hotel in the main square, detached a squad of men to locate Mr. Boyd's room, and there deliberately murdered him, putting two bullets through his forehead, and several through other parts of his body . . . on

account of the fact that Mr. Boyd was the prosecuting attorney of Greene County, Alabama and he was prosecuting persons charged with Ku-Klux outrages. . . . No effort was made to arrest the murderers, although the sheriff was at the hotel soon after the murder. The town was full of strangers, but they did nothing as they were terrorized by the ruffians. Mr. Boyd was buried the next day, but not one of his legal brethren attended his funeral.

Cox goes on to give an account of some of the one hundred murders and thousands of acts of violence and what he calls "intimidation and terrorism" perpetrated by the Ku Klux Klan that led to key pieces of US federal legislation in 1871 that condemned "force, intimidation, or threat" and provided civil and criminal penalties intended to deal with conspiratorial violence of the kind practiced by the Klan. Deriving the first two parts of their name from the Greek *kýklos* (meaning "circle" or "band") and the last part from the Scottish and English word *clan*, the Ku Klux Klan has existed in some form since six college-educated Confederate veterans— John C. Lester, John B. Kennedy, James R. Crowe, Frank O. McCord, Richard R. Reed, and J. Calvin Jones—founded the group in the town of Pulaski, Tennessee on Christmas Eve of 1865. Composed mostly of Southern Civil War veterans still steeped in the ideals of the Confederacy, by the end of the nineteenth century the KKK grew from a quasi-secret society into a full-blown paramilitary force hell bent on reversing the Reconstruction and preserving the heritage of the South, which included viewing African-Americans as slaves. The KKK engaged in terrorist raids against African-Americans, white Reconstructionist Republicans, and carpetbaggers (Yankees who transplanted to the South) at night in their little white hoodies using methods such as torture, assault, intimidation, as well as firebombing, blasting, shooting, lynching, and other forms of murder to intimidate, threaten, or terrorize people. A government report sent to Washington, DC, from Tennessee's chapter of the Freedmen's Bureau in 1868 concluded: "The Ku Klux organization is so extensive, and so well organized and armed, that it is beyond the power of anyone to exert any moral influence over them. Powder and ball is the only thing that will put them down."

The Haymarket Riot

In the early 1800s, a normal workweek in the US (and practically all of the other industrialized countries) was fourteen to sixteen hours a day, seven days a week. Because owners and managers could get away with paying them next to nothing for their work, women and children were often employed. Here's an entry from a precocious thirteen-year-old girl's diary, dated September 20th 1856 (which was a Sunday, by the way). She worked at a textile mill in Lowell, Massachusetts:

Dear Diary,

Today I got up at 5.15am. For breakfast I had a piece of left over bread from yesterday. I already feel tired because I got back late, and now I'm up early. I got to work at 5.45am. I wish I had some nice clothes to wear because my clothes are ripped and dirty. By the time I got to work I was in trouble because I was five minutes late. I always feel hungry because Mom doesn't have enough for all of us, and we're always starving. Sometimes we have to steal food because we are really hungry. I do not like the overseer because he sits there, while we are working really hard. I got in trouble at work because I lost my shoe and I made one from their material. My friend, Lucy, got in trouble today because she didn't wash. The punishment was 6 whips on her back, one after the other—it was so painful because Lucy cried for the next hour, and I don't blame her! I could not watch because the sounds were horrible. I can't even believe the sight . . . I left work at 10.15pm, but I can't sleep now even though I know I must . . .

By the mid-1800s workers in the major cities of the US formed unions and went on strike, negotiating with factory owners, bankers, managers, and merchants for a ten-hour workday, then a nine-hour day. On May 3rd 1886 the Chicago police killed two demonstrators who were part of a group of workers striking for an eight-hour workday. One day later, on May 4th, the bloodshed continued. Some one thousand demonstrators stood in a light rain at Haymarket Square in Chicago to listen to labor leader, August Spies, talk about workers' rights and the need for an eight-hour day. Near the end of the demonstration, as the Chicago police were trying to disperse the crowd, someone threw a homemade, dynamite-filled, sphere-shaped bomb at the police, which exploded killing seven of them. The police then fired into the crowd, and people in the crowd fired back—four people from the crowd were killed and some seventy others wounded, while sixty police officers were wounded. In the aftermath, eight labor leaders dubbed anarchists and socialists were charged, tried, and found guilty. Seven were sentenced to hang, to include August Spies, and one received a life sentence. According to witnesses, in the moments before he was hanged, Spies shouted, "The time will come when our silence will be more powerful than the voices you strangle today!"

Bombing of the *Los Angeles Times* Building

It was called "The Crime of the Century." In the late 1880s, steel had virtually replaced wood and stone in the construction of buildings and bridges, and the number of skyscrapers, along with the number of ironworkers falling to their deaths, increased exponentially in the major cities of the US, primarily in New York, Chicago, and Los Angeles. Mainly because of the long hours doing this kind of dangerous work, ironworkers formed unions and often went on strike, picketing construction sites and other places. Los Angeles had the reputation of being the most militantly anti-union city in America—in fact, the Merchants and Manufacturers Association in LA claimed to have one creed: "We will employ no union man." Pickets were generally orderly and little violence occurred in LA until July 15th 1910, when LA's City Council passed its infamous anti-picketing ordinance. Fights and arrests were a regular occurrence for the rest of the summer. At around 1:07 A.M. on October 1st 1910, a bomb went off in an alley outside the three-story *Los Angeles Times* building located at First Street and Broadway in LA. The bomb was supposed to go off at 4:00 A.M. when the building would have been empty, but the clock timing mechanism apparently was faulty. The sixteen sticks of dynamite in the suitcase bomb were enough to collapse the side of the *Times* building, and the fire afterwards destroyed it completely along with the building next door that housed the paper's. Of the 115 people in the *Times* building that evening, twenty-one died, with most being burned alive. Brothers John J. McNamara and James B. McNamara, both members of the LA chapter of the International Association of Bridge and Structural Iron Workers, were tried and convicted of the crime, spending years in prison before both dying in 1941. There were actually numerous bombings all over the country during the turn of the twentieth century, usually perpetrated by workers characterized by the media as "midnight assassins," "cowardly murderers," "leeches upon honest labor," and "anarchic scum." After the bombing, one of the founding members of Industrial Workers of the World and probably the most important member of the Socialist Party of America, Eugene Debs (1855–1926), noted in a letter to a friend that the McNamara brothers "were the products of Capitalism." Continuing in the letter:

> If you want to judge McNamara you must first serve a month as a structural ironworker on a skyscraper, risking your life every minute to feed your wife and babies, then being discharged and blacklisted for joining a union. Every floor in every skyscraper represents a workingman killed in its erection. It is easy enough for a gentleman of education and refinement to sit at his typewriter and point out the crimes of the workers. But let him be one of them himself, reared in hard poverty, denied education, thrown into the brute struggle for existence from childhood, oppressed, exploited, forced to strike, clubbed by the police, jailed while his family is evicted, and his wife and children are hungry, and he will hesitate to

condemn these as criminals who fight against the crimes of which they are the victims of such savage methods as have been forced upon them by their masters.

The 1920 Wall Street Bombing

Remember. We will not tolerate any longer. Free the political prisoners or it will be death for all of you. American Anarchist Fighters!

This was written on a note that a mail carrier found in a mailbox a block away from the J.P. Morgan bank headquarters in downtown Manhattan, New York at 23 Wall Street just minutes before 100 pounds of dynamite and 500 pounds of cast-iron slugs exploded across the street from the bank at around noon on September 16th 1920, killing thirty immediately, injuring hundreds of others, overturning cars and carriages, and blowing out the windows of buildings for blocks away. The terrorists obviously knew that around noon is when the most people would be on the street taking a break for lunch, and they also apparently wanted to make a statement condemning capitalism. Within the coming months, some ten more people would of wounds inflicted that day, and the damage would be estimated in the millions. The *Daily Call*, a newspaper of the Socialist Party of America, reported: "The horrible slaughter and maiming of men and women was a calamity that almost stills the beating of the heart of the people." No one was ever caught. In 2002, comparing the events of 9/11 to the 1920 Wall Street bombing, Beverly Gage noted:

> When Americans in 1920 heard of the carnage on Wall Street, many believed they had encountered a type of violence never before seen. There had been bomb explosions before—at Chicago's Haymarket Square in 1886, at the *Los Angeles Times* building in 1910—but they had been part of specific labor disputes, party to specific protests. The blast on Wall Street, by contrast, seemed to be purely symbolic, designed to kill as many innocent people as possible in an assault on American power.

At the time, J.P. Morgan bank probably was the most well-known and important banks in American finance, and many have speculated that the bombing was perpetrated either by anarchists, socialists, or communists, all groups that despised American capitalism and free trade and that were especially active during the early part of the twentieth century. The FBI closed the case in 1940, having no suspects. To this day, the façade of the old Morgan building still has indentations and round, inward, pock-marked domes on the limestone. J.P. Morgan himself in 1920, and the corporate bodies of the Morgan Company since, have all made it clear that they will never repair the damage, in defiance to those who committed the act and as a symbol of American economic freedom and resilience.

Bath School Bombing and Murder-Suicide

It seemed as though the school's floor went up several feet from the explosion . . . Mother after mother came running into the school yard, and demanded information about her child and, on seeing the lifeless form lying on the lawn, sobbed and swooned... In no time, more than 100 men were at work tearing away the debris of the school, and nearly as many women were frantically pawing over the timber and broken bricks for traces of their children.

A school board member named Andrew Kehoe caused all of this, believe it or not. Kehoe was an arrogant, angry, abusive, intolerant, violent man who managed to get elected in 1924 as treasurer of the Bath Consolidated School Board in the small town of Bath, Michigan. He lost the position in 1926, telling his neighbor, "They'll pay . . . they'll all pay." With his house and farm in foreclosure and his wife dying of tuberculosis, over the course of the summer months of 1926 Kehoe not only beat one of his horses to death and killed all of the trees, bushes, shrubs, grapevines, plants, and crops on his land through various means, but he also lined his homestead, his truck, and Bath Elementary School with several hundred pounds of dynamite, shrapnel, and pyrotol, an

incendiary explosive used by farmers at that time for exca-
vation and burning of debris. On the morning of May 18th
1927, classes at Bath Elementary began at 8:30. By then,
Kehoe had already murdered his wife, placed her body in a
wheelbarrow, and burned her corpse. He also had packed
more dynamite, shrapnel, and pyrotol into his 1925 Ford
Model T truck and was driving to the elementary school. At
around 8:35 A.M. the bombs he placed around his homestead
went off, and people began rushing to his farm. At about 8:45
A.M., in the basement of the north wing of the school, an
alarm clock set by Kehoe detonated the dynamite, shrapnel,
and pyrotol he had hidden there, killing thirty children and
eight adults, and wounding another fifty children and eight
adults. In the midst of all of the blood, body parts, screaming,
and confusion, Kehoe showed up at the school in his truck,
summoned Superintendent Emory Huyck over to the truck,
then fired a shot into the truck causing the dynamite to explode, killing Huyck, himself, two other men, and an eight-
year-old boy who had wandered out of the school... There's
likely a special spot in Hell where Kehoe now resides.

The First Act of Air Sabotage in the History of Commercial Aviation

Our investigation convinced me that the tragedy resulted from an
explosion somewhere in the region of the baggage compartment
in the rear of the plane. Everything in front of the compartment was
blown forward, everything behind blown backward, and things at
the side outward.

So noted the lead investigator at the Chicago Bureau of Investigation in his report about a United Airlines Boeing 247
mid-air explosion that occurred on October 10th 1933 over
Chesterston, Indiana, killing all seven on board. Witnesses
reported hearing an explosion and looking to the skies
around 9 P.M. to see what looked like a fiery comet crashing
to the ground. The tail section of the plane was discovered
nearly intact about a mile away from the rest of the wreck-

age. No one was ever caught, and the case remains unsolved. This is thought to be the first proven act of air sabotage in the history of commercial aviation.

The Mad Bomber

CON EDISON CROOKS—THIS IS FOR YOU

That's what the note said that was left with a home-made pipe bomb in a wooden toolbox and placed on a NYC Consolidated Edison power plant window sill in 1940. It was placed there by George P. Metesky (1903–1994), AKA, the Mad Bomber. That bomb never went off, but of the thirty-three, or so, pipe bombs that Metesky placed in the seat cushions of NYC theaters, phone booths, storage lockers, mail boxes, subways, toilets, and restrooms in places such as the NYC Public Library, Port Authority, Grand Central Station, Pennsylvania Station, RCA Building, and Radio City Music Hall between 1940 and 1956, twenty-two of them did go off injuring some fifteen people. Although no one was killed by the bombs, many had their arses torched since Metesky's main M.O. was to conceal the bombs where folks would sit—comfy chairs or even toilets! Metesky was pissed at Con Edison because he lost his job after twenty-six weeks of collecting sick pay due to a boiler accident in 1931.

Metesky tried to sue Con Edison, claiming the accident led to pneumonia and tuberculosis, but lost and blamed Con Edison's lawyers and a few workers who testified in favor of Con Edison for his misfortunes. Metesky would often place the pipe bombs in a wool sock, at times hanging the sock from something secure. In fact, people were told to be on the lookout for wool socks, especially ones hanging in bizarre locations. Not long after a bomb scare at the Empire State Building in 1956, a Con Edison clerk named Alice Kelly started looking through transcripts of reports of disgruntled employees from before World War II and noticed that Metesky used the words *dastardly deeds* several times during his litigation against Con Edison between 1931 and

1936—she also noticed that the Mad Bomber used these words, too, after reading Mad Bomber letters published in the newspaper. This led to Metesky's arrest on January 21st 1957, the discovery of several mismatched wool socks and lots of bomb-making stuff, a confession by Metesky claiming that he had perpetrated his own dastardly deeds because he felt Con Edison gave him a "bum deal," and a sixteen-year trip to Matteawan Hospital for the Criminally Insane in Beacon, New York. The day he got out in 1973, Metesky claimed in an interview: "I wrote 900 letters to the Mayor, to the Police Commissioner, to the newspapers, and I never even got a penny postcard back. Then I went to the newspapers to try to buy advertising space, but all of them turned me down. I was compelled to bring my story to the public."

Weathermen Bombings, Sabotage, Theft, and Murder

"More Body Parts Discovered in Debris of Blast on 11th Street" was the title of a news article in the *New York Times* from March 16th 1970. It was referring to an explosion that occurred in a Greenwich Village townhouse on March 6th 1970 that "reduced the four-story townhouse to a burning rubble-strewn ruin." Three persons preparing several pipe bombs taped with nails were blown into pieces instantly, and two others were injured but escaped from the scene—police had to identify the persons killed through dental records. All involved were members of an American extremist left-wing group called the Weather Underground Organization, or simply the Weathermen, that formed sometime in the summer of 1969 as a splinter group of University of Michigan students in direct response to the Vietnam War and numerous US government actions that they perceived as being unjust. Their name supposedly is derived from a line in Bob Dylan's song, "Subterranean Homesick Blues": "You don't need a weatherman to know which way the wind blows."

By the fall of 1969, the Weathermen decided to go underground so as to "engage in guerilla warfare against the US government," as noted in one FBI report. From 1969 to 1981, their numbers ranged anywhere from three to three hundred, and the typical Weathermen MO was bombing of facilities, but almost always warning folks to evacuate before the bombs went off. They started bombing Chicago Police cars in 1969, then engaged in several bombings during 1970, to include blowing up parts of the San Francisco Police Department headquarters, NYC Police headquarters, NYC Bank of America headquarters, the National Guard in DC, the Presidio in SFC, several courthouses around the country, and other monuments, statues, and memorials. On March 1st 1971, they bombed a bathroom in the US Capitol claiming it was "in protest of the US invasion of Laos." On May 19th 1972—the eighty-second birthday of Ho Chi Minh, Communist leader of North Vietnam—they bombed a bathroom in the Pentagon as "retaliation for the US bombing raid in Hanoi." For the January 29th 1975 bombing of the United States Department of State building, they stated that it was "in response to escalation in Vietnam." In 2008 one of the founders of the Weathermen, Bill Ayers, noted in an interview: "The Weather Underground went on to take responsibility for placing several small bombs in empty offices. . . . We did carry out symbolic acts of extreme vandalism directed at monuments to war and racism, and the attacks on property—never on people—were meant to respect human life and convey outrage and determination to end the Vietnam War." Ayers went on to a career in writing, education, and academia—believe it or not—and retired as a professor at the University of Illinois at Chicago, College of Education. During his Friday night radio program on August 29th 2008, speaking about Ayers and the Weathermen, Mark Levin laid out this list of Weathermen terrorist activities:

> 7th October 1969. Bombing of Haymarket Police Statue in Chicago, apparently as a kickoff for the Days of Rage riots in the city.

6th December 1969. Bombing of several Chicago Police cars parked in a precinct parking lot at 3600 North Halsted Street, Chicago.

27th–31st December 1969. Weathermen hold a War Council meeting in Flint, Michigan, where they finalize their plans to submerge into an underground status from which they plan to commit strategic acts of sabotage against the government. Thereafter they are called the Weather Underground Organization (WUO).

13th February 1970. Bombing several police vehicles of the Berkeley, California, Police Department.

16th February 1970. Bombing of Golden Gate Park branch of the San Francisco Police Department, killing one officer and injuring a number of other policemen.

6th March 1970. Bombing in the 13th Police District of the Detroit, Michigan.

6th March 1970. "Bomb Factory" located in New York's Greenwich Village accidentally explodes. Three WUO members die. The bomb was intended to be planted at a non-commissioned officer's dance at Fort Dix, New Jersey. The bomb was packed with nails to inflict maximum casualties on detonation.

30th March 1970. Chicago Police discover a WUO bomb factory on Chicago's north side; a few days later a WUO weapons cache is discovered on Chicago's south side.

10th May 1970. Bombing of The National Guard Association building in Washington, DC.

21st May 1970. The WUO under Bernardine Dohrn's (Bill Ayers' current wife) name releases its "Declaration of a State of War" communiqué.

9th June 1970. Bombing of New York City Police Headquarters.

7th July 1970. Bombing of The Presidio army base in San Francisco. [report in *The New York Times*, 7/27/70]

12th September 1970. The WUO helps Dr. Timothy Leary break out and escape from the California Men's Colony prison.

8th October 1970. Bombing of Marin County courthouse. [*New York Times*, 8/10/70]

10th October 1970. Bombing of Queens, NY traffic-court building. [*New York Times*, 10/10/70]

14th October 1970. Bombing of Harvard Center for International Affairs. [*New York Times*, 10/14/70]

1st March 1971. Bombing of US Capitol. [*New York Times*, 3/2/71]

April 1971. Abandoned WUO bomb factory discovered in San Francisco.

29th August 1971. Bombing of Office of California Prisons. [*New York Times*, 8/29/71]

17th September 1971. Bombing Department of Corrections, Albany, NY. [*New York Times*, 9/18/71]

5th October 1971. Bombing of William Bundy's office at MIT. [*New York Times*, 10/16/71]

19th May 1972. Bombing of Pentagon. [*New York Times*, 5/19/72]

18th May 1973. Bombing of the 103rd Police Precinct in New York.

28th September 1973. Bombing of ITT headquarters in New York and Rome. [*New York Times*, 9/28/73]

6th March 1974. Bombing of Health, Education and Welfare offices in San Francisco.

31st May 1974. Bombing of Office of the California Attorney General.

17th June 1974. Bombing of Gulf Oil's Pittsburgh head-quarters.

11th September 1974. Bombing of Anaconda Corporation.

29th January 1975. Bombing of the US State Department.

16th June 1975. Bombing of Banco de Ponce Bank in New York.

September 1975. Bombing of the Kennecott Corporation.

20th October 1981. Brinks robbery near Nyack, New York, where $1 million was stolen, two police officers and one Brinks guard were murdered, and several others wounded.

In a *New York Times* interview from 2001, Ayers claimed: "I don't regret setting bombs. I feel we didn't do enough."

Anti-Abortionists

"If I hear you are still killing when I get to town, I will haunt you and your wife day and night and give you no peace. If you continue, I will hunt you down like any other wild beast and kill you . . ." The threat letter communicating this was typed on unusual stationery that featured a cloudburst with lightning. It was typed by a twenty-two-year-old militant, fanatical anti-abortionist from Oregon named Angela Shannon, and in March of 1994 was placed in the mailbox of Dr. George Woodward, a physician who performed abortions at a Planned Parenthood clinic in Milwaukee, Wisconsin. Angela went to prison for almost four years for this threat.

Several months earlier, in August of 1993, Angela's mother, Shelly Shannon, shot late-term abortionist Dr. George Tiller once in each arm outside his clinic in Wichita, Kansas. "I deny that it was wrong," wrote Shelly in a letter to her daughter about the shooting while in jail, "It was the most holy, most righteous thing I've ever done. I have no regrets. I hope he's not killing babies today." Tiller was used to the craziness, actually, as a pipe bomb which caused more than $70,000 in damages exploded at his clinic in June of 1986.

Tragically, Tiller had half of his head blown off on May 31st 2009 by anti-abortion activist Scott Roeder during worship services at the Reformation Lutheran Church in Wichita, where he was serving as an usher and handing out church bulletins. In the US between 1993 and 2009, radical anti-abortionists have killed four doctors, two clinic employees, a security guard, and a clinic escort. Since 1984, numerous abortion doctors and people at abortion clinics have been spat on, urinated on, stabbed, hacked with axes, shot, blown up, and had acid thrown on them, and abortion clinics have been spat on, urinated on, vandalized, graffiti-ed, firebombed with Molotov cocktails, blown up, and rammed into with cars.

The Army of God is a militant anti-abortionist terrorist organization that fully supports killing abortionists. "This is why the shooting of babykilling abortionist George Tiller was Justifiable Homicide" is what one finds when clicking on their website, along with a slideshow of aborted fetuses. A copy of "The Army of God Manual" was discovered in Shelly Shannon's backyard after she shot Tiller with the following words underlined in the Declaration at the beginning: "We do officially declare war on the entire child killing industry . . . your pagan, heathen, infidel souls . . . we begged you to stop, but you mocked God and continued the Holocaust . . . All of the options have expired. Our Most Dread Sovereign Lord God requires that whosoever sheds man's blood, by man shall his blood be shed. Not out of hatred of you, but out of love for the persons you exterminate, we are forced to take arms against you."

The Unabomber

I started work on my PhD in philosophy in August of 1996 at Saint Louis University, some four months after Ted Kaczynski, the confessed Unabomber, was arrested—so, his heinous crimes were on the minds of most folks in the US. Besides teaching, one job I had as a TA my first year was to pick up the mail for the philosophy department from the vestibule of the Humanities Building. I'll never forget the beat up, over-taped, brown-paper-wrapped, shoe-box-sized package I received one fall day with no return address and my name scrawled in pen on it, and how I paused to think, "My God, what if this is a bomb?" I left it in the vestibule and called my sister back in Chicago, who would periodically send me things in the mail. "Yes, Robert," she said, "I had Jim (her husband) ship it from his warehouse." To which I responded, "Well, it scared the sh@t out of me because it didn't have a return address on it, and it looks like something the Unabomber would send!" It was cookies she had sent as a kind of "Happy Start of Grad School" gift.

It wasn't cookies that a policeman on the campus of the University of Illinois at Chicago discovered in May of 1978 when he opened a suspicious package, however; rather, it was an exploding homemade pipe bomb that burned him, damaged his eardrum, and sent shrapnel deep into his left hand. It could have been worse since the pipe was sealed with wooden ends, rather than the typical threaded metal caps that would have caused a bigger blast. This was the first of fifteen bombs that Ted Kaczynski would mail to unsuspecting victims. Kaczynski is serving a life sentence for killing three people and injuring twenty-three in a nationwide series of mail bombs (and one airplane bomb) sent between 1978 and 1995. By 1981, Kaczynski had mailed three bombs that went off—one to a university professor, one to a grad student, and one to the President of United Airlines—and planted one bomb on an airplane that exploded mid-flight. Fortunately, no one was killed. Because of these UNiversity and Airline BOMbs, the FBI started referring to the manhunt for the bomber as the UNABOM case, so the media picked it up and started calling this person the Unabomber. By 1995, three people had been killed by his bombs—a computer storeowner (1985), an advertising executive (1994), and a timber industry lobbyist (1995). The last person blown up after opening a package addressed to him in his office was a guy named Gilbert B. Murray, an official of the California Forestry Association, who was married with two kids. "The bomb so badly destroyed Gil Murray's body," wrote one of Kaczynski's prosecutors, "that his family was allowed only to see and touch his feet and legs, below the knees, as a final farewell."

By then, Kaczynski had realized that by taping numerous razor blades and nails to the bomb, the shrapnel would inflict more damage. A Harvard-trained former professor with near-genius-level ability in mathematics (believe it or not), Kaczynski was apparently pissed off at the progress made in science and technology as a result of the Industrial Revolution, and how such progress has de-humanized and alienated people. A read of what has been called the Unabomber Manifesto—a document titled "Industrial Society and Its Future" written by Kaczynski in 1995—is kind of all over the place in terms of its main point and reeks of "This guy is ranting and is F-ing nuts." Kaczynski sent it to *The New York Times* and *The Washington Post*, and *The Post* published it in 1995, where it was seen by Kaczynski's brother, who contacted the FBI. In one of his journal entries from the late 1970s, Kaczynski wrote: "I emphasize that my motivation is personal revenge. I don't pretend any kind of philosophical or moralistic justification." In another from 1982, he wrote that he was frustrated: "I can't seem to make a lethal bomb."

After his first deadly attack in 1985 in Sacramento, California killed computer storeowner Hugh Scrutton, Kaczynski joyfully journaled: "Excellent. Humane way to eliminate somebody. He probably never felt a thing." In their arguments at Kaczynski's trial, the prosecutors provided an account of the second person to be killed by one of Kaczynski's bombs, Thomas Mosser: "Thomas opened the package; the ensuing blast drove shrapnel into his body, leaving a gaping hole in his head, opening his body and piercing his organs with nails. He died at age fifty on the floor of his own home, his wife at his side trying in vain to aid and comfort him."

Expendable Assets

ROBERT ARP, PHD, used to be a professional philosopher, but now works as an analyst for the US Government. He *could* tell you what he does for the Govies, . . . but then he really would have to kill you.

ADAM BARKMAN, PHD, is Associate Professor of Philosophy and Chair of the Department of Philosophy at Redeemer University College in Canada. He is the author and co-editor of more than half a dozen books, most recently *Imitating the Saints* (2013) and *The Culture and Philosophy of Ridley Scott* (2013). Unlike his grandfather (or nearly every character on *Homeland*), Adam hasn't had a gun waved in his face by a hostile force in a foreign land, but he *has* faced down the wagging tongues of angry, middle-aged academics from neighboring universities and so does have claim to, if not the better part, at least the crumbs of courage.

DAN BURKETT hails from New Zealand, but is currently stationed on foreign soil as a philosophy PhD student at Rice University in Houston, Texas. He specializes in morality, freedom, the philosophy of time, and brainwashing others into accepting his philosophical arguments.

DONA CAYETANA is finishing her PhD at the University of Melbourne in English and Cultural Studies with a dissertation on the representation of women in post-9/11 fiction. She works undercover investigating the connections between contemporary politics and textual forms.

CHRISTIAN COTTON is Instructor of Philosophy and Religion at Piedmont College and nearly completed with his PhD in philosophy. With interests in anarchism and radical environmental philosophy, he's pretty sure he's on any number of government watch lists, and it wouldn't surprise him if they had eyes and ears on him as well. Hey, it's not paranoia if they *really are* after you!

IAN DIORIO is a pastor and adjunct professor at Hope International University. He holds a doctorate in leadership, but he's pretty sure the CIA won't be offering him a job anytime soon.

NATHAN EVERSON is currently undertaking a Masters of Research in Philosophy through Macquarie University doing work in animal ethics in Continental philosophy, as well as philosophy of work and labor. Nathan is currently employed as a forklift operator.

Much like Raqim Faisel, **DON FALLIS, PHD**, is a covert operative who pretends to be merely a mild-mannered college professor. . . . In fact, maybe he isn't even a professor of Information Resources and an adjunct professor of Philosophy at the University of Arizona at all. After all, he lists *lying* and *deception* as his areas of expertise.

JOHN R. FITZPATRICK, PHD, is a lecturer in philosophy at the University of Tennessee, Chattanooga teaching primarily in the history of philosophy and ethics. He is the author of *John Stuart Mill's Political Philosophy: Balancing Freedom and the Collective Good* (2006) and *Starting with Mill* (2010) as well as a contributor to several works on popular culture and philosophy. He is also a life member of the United States Chess Federation, and he would like to tell you all about this—but, unfortunately it's classified.

JAI GALLIOTT, JP, is a philosopher at Macquarie University in Sydney, Australia. He thinks he's a spy, therefore he is, right?

JASON IULIANO received his **JD** from Harvard Law School and is currently a PhD candidate in Politics at Princeton University where he's writing a dissertation on the metaphysics of corporate personhood. While in law school, he mastered the art of highlighting information in different colors and drawing connections between seemingly unrelated cases. With these skills in hand, Jason feels prepared to challenge Carrie to an Evidence Corkboard Faceoff.

EDWIN DANIEL JACOB is a doctoral student of Global Affairs at Rutgers University. His research on the ethics and efficacy of emergent military technologies has yet to be declassified.

LÁSZLÓ KAJTÁR is doctoral candidate in philosophy at Central European University, Budapest, and is interested in storytelling. . . . Or, at least that's his cover story.

xifo tqpuufe po uif tusffut pg dijdbhp cz wbsjpvt hpwfsonfou bhfout, gpsfjho tqjft, boe tibepxz of''fs-ep-xfmmt, boe btlfe qpjou-cmbol jg if jt "uif" **JOHN V. KARAVITIS, CPA, MBA**, xip xsjuft fttbzt jo qpqvmbs dvmuvsf boe qijmptpqiz cpplt, kpio bmxbzt sftqpoet uibu uifsf jt "op-tvdi-bvuips," boe tubsst xbmljoh gbtufs. nvdi gbtufs.

BRITTANY LORENZ is an independent scholar working in Ottawa, Canada, to make certain that Canadian policies (political science) have roots in ethics (philosophy). After her childhood dream of being one of the X-Men was crushed, she's come to realize that she has a better chance of taking down the Hellfire Club (and other terrorist organizations) through more legitimate government channels.

APRIL MARRATTO is currently working on her MA in philosophy at Trinity Western University in Canada—and her political science friends never let her forget it. She's also a Canadian spy embedded deep in the US doing surveillance on . . . Wait, did we just say that out loud?

TRIP MCCROSSIN teaches in the Philosophy Department at Rutgers University, where he works on, among other things, the nature, history, and legacy of the Enlightenment. His chapter in the book is part of a broader effort to view literary and other forms of popular culture through the lens of Susan Neiman's understanding of the same. He sometimes dreams of the student who would say to themselves, in preparing their next assignment, "I missed something once before; I won't, I can't, let that happen again."

TALIA MORAG, PhD, is a lecturer of philosophy and psychoanalysis at the University of Sydney. She considers herself a double agent, having a hand in both Anglo-American and Continental traditions of philosophy.

A strict deontologist, **WILLIAM RODRIGUEZ, PHD**, has been known to associate—on the very, very, very rare occasion—with utilitarians and consequentialists. He spends every waking moment trying to turn relativists (and possibly a few foreign spies) to his absolutist brand of philosophy.

FRANK SCALAMBRINO, PHD, is an affiliate assistant professor at the University of Dallas. His work in metaphysics and philosophy of psychology has been characterized as a *critique of terroristic reason*.

ROBERTO SIRVENT, PHD, is Associate Professor of Political and Social Ethics at Hope International University. He hopes this book doesn't get him deported.

Index